SAND IN MY SHOES

Sand in My Shoes

*Reflections from Somalia on the Environment,
Violence, and Development*

JONATHAN RUDY

RESOURCE *Publications* • Eugene, Oregon

SAND IN MY SHOES
Reflections from Somalia on the Environment, Violence, and Development

Resource Publications
An Imprint of Wipf and Stock Publishers
199 W. 8th Ave., Suite 3
Eugene, OR 97401

www.wipfandstock.com

PAPERBACK ISBN: 978-1-6667-7767-3
HARDCOVER ISBN: 978-1-6667-7768-0
EBOOK ISBN: 978-1-6667-7769-7

02/23/24

All photographs are from the personal collection of Jonathan Edward Rudy.

All poetry was written by Jonathan Edward Rudy.

*For Solomon and David who, by osmosis,
have been shaped by this story*

Contents

My Chronological/ Geographical Phases

Beginning to Breathe Phase

1960 – September: Born in Ontario, Canada

1960 – 2 weeks after birth moved to Indiana –lived 3 places, South Bend, Elkhart, Ft. Wayne

1967 – moved to Columbia, South Carolina

1968 – moved to New Holland, Pennsylvania

1969 – moved to Smithville, Ohio

1975 – moved to La Junta, Colorado

1977 – moved to Harrisonburg, Virginia – last year of high school in the dorms there

Electronics Geek Phase

1978 – moved to Phoenix, Arizona

1980 – began a year aboard the *Anne Bravo*, seismic research vessel starting in Houston for orientation, then to the Bering Sea, Southern California, and US Gulf Coast

1982 – moved to Goshen, Indiana for college

1983 – fall, study abroad in Chengdu, Sichuan, China

1984 – married Carolyn

International Development Phase

1985 – moved to North Newton, Kansas –to finish undergrad

1987 – moved to Somalia for volunteer service with Mennonite Central Committee –Hargeisa, Geddo, Kismayo, Mogadishu

1987 – language study in Garissa, Kenya –6 weeks

1989 – left Somalia for the last time 13 Sept.

Reacquainting with Myself Phase

1989 – moved to La Junta, Colorado

Program Administrator Phase

1993 – moved to Mbabane, Swaziland –now Eswatini– as country reps, visited 6 countries in Southern Africa for 1 month writing histories of Mennonites in the region

Anabaptist Theologian Phase

1999 – moved to Harrisonburg, Virginia for grad studies

2001 – moved to Davao City, Mindanao, Philippines as regional peace resource person for MCC traveling to 20 countries in the greater Asia Region

Peace Consultant Phase

2007 – moved to Manheim, Pennsylvania

2007 – Philippine relational connections for MCC and CDA project work x 2 through 2009

2008 – Kenya Program review for MCC

2009 – South Sudan admin support for MCC

2011 – Burkina Faso admin support for MCC

2011 – Afghanistan 11-month –109 days in 4 trips– peace mentor with Oxfam

Professor in Higher Education & Human Security* Phase

2012 – started Peacemaker in Residence job at Elizabethtown College –during this tenure there I traveled to Philippines (x9), Holland (x3), Switzerland (x2), Austria, Ireland, Italy, Thailand, Gambia, Zanzibar-Tanzania

2013 – began regular trips to Somaliland (x8)

2014 – began work in Lao PDR (x4)

2015 – began as Alliance for Peacebuilding Senior Advisor –later Fellow– for Human Security

2016 – Fulbright specialist placement in Pune, Maharashtra, India

2018 – South Sudan Program review for MCC

2019 – Northeast Asia/Korean Program review for MCC

2019 – Ended Peacemaker in Residence job at Elizabethtown College

2020 – Egypt Program review for MCC

2021 – Peacebuilding Program Review for IAM in Afghanistan

*While somewhat overlapping, the last 13 years I have traveled all over Africa and Asia and Europe for consulting work, sitting on airplanes between 120–200 hours a year doing peace and human security trainings

Memoir Writer Phase

2019–2020 Writing this memoir

Peace Educator Design Phase

2020 August – Present – Reaffirmation that I am an educator in peacebuilding, conflict transformation, nonviolence, human security, and peace education design

Map of the Horn of Africa

- Hargeisa/Saba'ad Refugee Camp – 1987 to 1988
- Garissa (Kenya) – 1987 for language Study
- Mogadishu – 1987 to 1989
- Kismayo – 1989

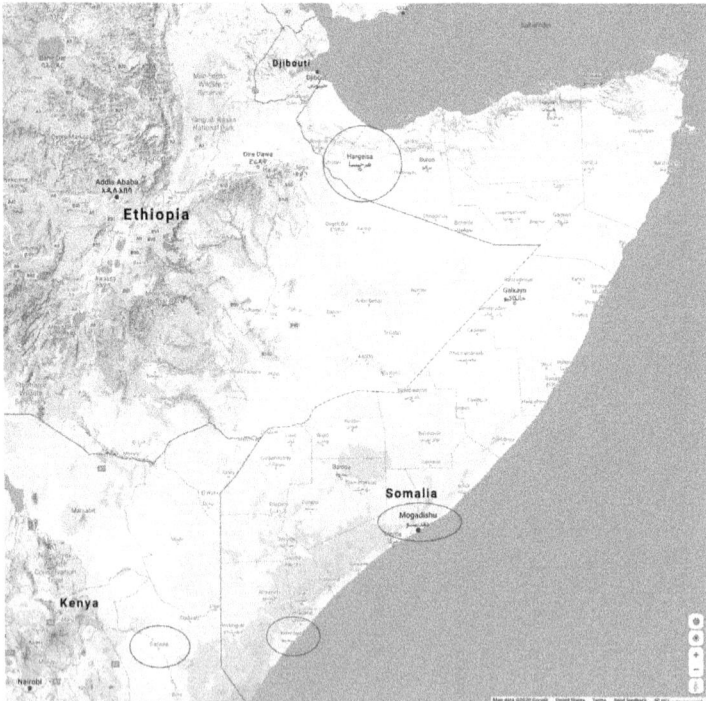

Acknowledgements

THIS BOOK IS WRITTEN for my sons Solomon and David. They have been inevitably shaped by this story even though it happened before they were born. The father I became to them was shaped by the sand swept tracks of bushland in Somalia.

Many people had a hand in this book, and I am eternally grateful for their careful, patient, and brutal kindness. Thanks go to Judy Bender Yoder, Jane Oswald Yoder, and Mary Zehr for their valuable proofing, seeing my typos and other errors.

Thanks to the Lancaster County Writers Meetup Group: Mel, Mike, and Susan. You all kept me focused and kept the micro and meta details on track. Special thanks to Diana Rico whose guidance, critique, and encouragement kept me believing this book is possible. A big thanks goes to Margaret High, who provided structural and copy editing.

Special thanks to my family who read drafts and gave advice and suggestions. Of mention is my son David, an excellent writer, who also spotted my typos and punctuation mistakes.

Finally, a big heart-filled thank you to my long-suffering friend, lover, and spouse Carolyn who shared these stories with me yet does not show up in this book until chapter 2. Carolyn and I were in the same place at the same time yet experienced totally different things. How is this possible that someone so near and dear is, at the same time excluded in much of my writing voice? I am discovering an uncomfortable paradox in penning a memoir. What I describe in my writing is an act of solitary remembrance. A true mystery among many I acknowledge exists in a big, wild, and complex thing called memory.

Introduction
Sand in My Shoes

"You get sand in your shoes from the first place you work internationally, and it doesn't come out."

Decades ago, I heard this truism spoken by a seasoned development expatriate, who coined the saying from a lifetime of work on the African continent. It has stuck with me all these years later. I suppose that is why, of all the numerous places I have lived and worked on four continents, Somaliland/Somalia holds such a fundamental intrigue for me. Somali sand, now integral to my life story, worked its way into my soul (sole!) and made a permanent home.

Sand is an irritant, an abrasive. On one hand, a small amount of sand can wreck machines and grind away the most hardened surface given enough time. On the other, sand is almost liquid, blowing in the wind and depositing into great ever- shifting dunes. Sand is the perfect metaphor for my engagement with Somalis over the past thirty-three years.

Friends have been encouraging me for years to write a book detailing these experiences in Somalia and other parts of the world where I was witness to the best and worst of humanity. They said that my accumulated experiences in exotic and conflicted places would make an interesting read. They said that the timing to be in places at historical significance would give a window into events that they only distantly got from the news. My response? "I am not old enough to write the book."

My patient partner, friend, and wife of 39 years Carolyn scolds me that this trope is too self-disrespecting. She names my favorite age-related quip of response to the question "What do you do for a living?" My self-deprecating answer is usually, "I don't know what I want to be when I grow up."

I suspect there is truth to her accusation. Yet, what I have done with my years in the workforce has been anything but a linear path. Most times I struggle to give the "elevator pitch" summary of my vocation because it's complicated and multifaceted. For example, I currently have at least a dozen involvements from training in peace education to helping a friend convert an old VW to electric. Some work pays $1000/day and other jobs I do *gratis*. Much of my work in the past decades has been volunteer.

The older I get the less I have to say, at least verbally. The linear models and symmetrical frameworks that gave me so much confidence a decade ago I am not as sure of now. What is relevant to carry the complexity of the world as it is today is poetry and short essays, hard won from experience. So, it seems timely that my inner compass routinely swings round to point in the direction of needing to tell *this* story.

In the summer of 2019, I lost my job. I was teaching peace and conflict studies at a small liberal arts college in central Pennsylvania. Hired in 2012 as the practical "conflict resolution guy" — in a program that had mostly political scientists, diplomats, and academics — I was to be the hands–on teaching part of the peace program.

It was seven years of lively engagement with students. With each class I taught, younger minds full of energy offered a fresh perspective and provided a sounding board that sifted my stories and experience to ever finer granules of clarity. Mustering my creativity while facilitating classroom learning experiences kept me connected with the frontiers of the peacebuilding field. I had funding for world travel that kept me engaged with peace practitioners while I provided international trainings on topics of human security, nonviolence, conflict transformation, reconciliation and inter-religious dialogue. This time period at the college was rich with accumulating more stories, but its intensity kept me from writing anything more than quick blog postings.

The forced reordering of higher education came with its budget cuts and program consolidation. Then came the Covid-19 lockdown. I finally had time to write the book. I wrote in essay form and poetry on the environment, violence, and security, primarily through the lens of my Somali experience.

Time Capsule

This is a story of self-discovery with help from the physical surroundings and the violent conflict I encountered. This is my quest to understand peace amidst a sometimes local and sometimes global failure to achieve it. As one who naturally sees patterns and symmetry, I find this is a messy business. Yet, looking back to the beginning of my international career, I wrote a paper in my college years that still feels truly relevant thirty-seven years later.

PC-212 Supplemental
Bethel College Class Paper
May 19, 1986
By Jon Rudy

This is the answer I came up with when a child asks me thirty years from now: "What did you do to make the world safe"?

I feel the sun beating down on my back. We used its creative, life-giving energy to do the things violent, unnatural human made energies used to do.

I hear the birds. They, by their songs, prompted us to stop using chemicals to destroy their food, insects. We now learn how nature does it and do what nature does to grow food.

I smell the breeze as it blows fresh air from the trees. We planted many more trees to replace what we destroyed. We don't need as many trees as we used to because we don't waste as much.

I touch the grass. It provides cover so our soil can stay healthy. We share food and water with others by not exploiting the land.

I see blue sky. We no longer clog the sky with pollution. We transformed the Military Industrial Complex into solar energy collection factories. They give us more energy than we know what to do with, so we let mother earth take what we don't need.

I taste the foods from 100 different countries. We don't have enemies now, just friends. Brothers and sisters come from all over the world to share their stories. They bring their recipes, and we give them ours.

I am struck by how clearly I named intersecting issues in this paper, seeing the connection between conflict/violence and the environment.

Old Letters

With ample time for Covid-compelled reflection, I went back to the primary source material of many of the stories found in the following pages. I spent hours sorting through a large stack of letters and aerograms. Both Carolyn's and my parents saved all the correspondence posted during our stay in Somalia from 1987 to 1989. Meticulously numbering each of her letters, Carolyn's mother set them aside with an almost reverent care. The numbering ascribed in letters to my parents was very hodgepodge, showing me how far back attention deficit and scattered thinking held sway on my behavior.

I carefully opened these letters, some of which were resealed by the humidity following their first opening. Carolyn's letters to her parents were in her own handwriting. My letters were almost entirely typewritten on old thunkety-thunkers with filled-in Os and slightly raised Gs. I find it difficult to decipher my own handwriting in those few letters that were done by my own pen.

I gathered as much of my writing as I could, 115,000 words in total and shoved it into this first-draft document. "There" I thought, "this is a great start." Sigh, memoir writing is nothing like that. It is more like surgery. Those beloved missives, which I thought at the time were word smithed so well, need invasive cutting not just a cosmetic touchup. To remove the warts on the page, each paragraph needed a fierce polishing, like sand burnishing the rough edges of my memory.

I dredged up old memories and brought them back into focus. By doing so I made myself so sick and tired of reliving those seminal times that I will be glad to be done with them. Once they're all written down on the page and bound up they will be parked on the shelves of my mind never to be seen again. Maybe that's the purpose of memoirs, to bracket things out, so they no longer shape, in a subconscious way, the motions of our arms and legs and being. Maybe that is the purpose of writing this book, to purge my gray matter of all that holds me. Perhaps that is why my friends thought I needed to write.

JONATHAN (JON) RUDY
Manheim, Pennsylvania, USA
6 October 2023

I

My Beginnings

Earliest Memory of Violence

During the tumultuous late 1960s when the US was burning with protests against the Vietnam/American war, while the halls of power were full of partisan mischief, and cities seethed with racial unrest, assassinations and chaotic riots, I had my earliest encounter with direct violence. It happened on the side of a snow-covered hill in Northeastern Ohio. I was the impressionable age of nine.

On that winter's day, a blanket of white lay thickly on the park near my home. I went out by myself to sled. I met another boy on the slope who was as tightly bundled up to ward off the cold as I was. To this day I am not sure who he was. It was so long ago that I only remember that this was my first, and only, full-bodied physical altercation. Somehow, we exchanged words. We threw snowballs in rage. Finally, we tussled in a fistfight softened by mittens. At the apex of our scuffle, we rolled down the hill, locked in tumbling hostility. The gloves, thick coats, and bulky boots meant that neither of us sustained any bruising blows.

The harm as I remember it was to my emotions. Violence had wrecked the possibility of fun, had soured my desire for sledding. But the biggest, most enduring memory is that I went home feeling immense guilt that I had been in a fist fight.

I was taught to love like Jesus and here I was with animosity in my heart and a skirmish on my conscience. The lesson for me from that day is how violence steals happiness and proliferates problems.

During those tumultuous late 60s this tussle on that winter's day was a microcosm of the wider world. The social unrest, from racial injustice to the war in the Mekong countries, was America's sledding hill.

As a child, I could not make sense of the wholesale slaughter going on in Southeast Asia. Every night the body count invaded our home on the evening news. It was always so lopsided: ten of them for one of ours. The Mennonite world I grew up in deeply shaped my response to global events. I was the son of a Mennonite pastor steeped in the words of Jesus, taken seriously by my faith community: "Love your enemies." My identity was forged in a tradition that maintained a stance of conscientious objection to military service and opted for alternative service to the country during times of war.

Political Conscientization

In 1972 when I was twelve, I bugged my sister's room. It happened during the silly season of politics. It was the chronological epicenter of the Watergate shenanigans, a time when politicians were bugging opponents' campaigns and spectacularly crashing out of politics from the abuse of power. As the national drama unfolded, I observed with the understanding of a child. By the time Tricky Dick (Richard Nixon) raised his short arms in a double V for victory sign while boarding the presidential helicopter for the last time, I was infected with political cynicism. It was the start of my political atheism and conscientization. It also had direct implications for my familial relationships.

The bugging was a simple enough scheme. I snaked thin wires from the clock radio perched on the headboard of my sister's bed down through the floor to my room below, amplifying the sound from her speaker and listening in to her "boy talk" whenever I wanted.

A couple of things amaze me as I look back on this clever yet unethical act. First, that I had the audacity to drill a hole through the floorboards of our house into her room for the wires to pass through and second, that my co-conspirator cousin and I figured out how to actually use the simple technology of the day to accomplish the spying. A third thing stuck with me as I look back all those years ago: how utterly uninteresting was the chatter of a teenage girl about boys and ponies and teen heart throbs like David Gates of the band *Bread* fame.

The demise of my short career in sibling espionage came at the hands of my brother who betrayed me to my sister. She rightly felt violated by this act, yet we remained connected throughout the years. With my brother, I had a back-yard tussle, the start of our becoming different people, paths in life diverging. The gulf between us took years to heal.

These antics of espionage were during a stable period of my childhood. Living five years in the same house was a novel thing by that stage in my life. This era was a calm between storms of geographical upheaval. So, I was influenced by, and to some degree, reflected the worlds around me. Listening in on my sister came from Watergate and the impeachment of Nixon. Building and launching Estes model rockets came from the Apollo lunar program. Rock-and-roll dovetailed with the rise in protest against the Vietnam/American war.

The church quietly taught competing values contrasting with the shrill voices from the news as these two worlds collided in my head. I was immersed in pop culture, affluence, militarism, and civil religion, which starkly contrasted with the pacifist Jesus-centric leanings of the Mennonite Church.

Peace Conscientization

In my teens our denomination was actively committed to conscientious objection to war. Our young men were doing alternative service in Atlanta, Colorado Springs, Gaborone, and Lusaka.

Dad was a Mennonite preacher in those days. In the heyday of that time in his life when he preached regularly, I sat through his sermons Sunday after Sunday. Surely he must have been addressing the national topics of conflict and peace. I don't know how many of those homilies I suffered through as a child, but to be honest, I can't remember the subject of any, save one. There is one word that stands out to me from a sermon Dad preached.

Sometime in the mid-1970s, in Smithville, Ohio, Dad's Sunday sermon focused on the concept of reconciliation. I remember being intrigued by that word. As a teen, bored with sitting still in church, perhaps it was the "silly" part of the word that tickled my fancy. Perhaps it was the communal resonance with reconciliation that caused it to affix itself to my grey matter. Whatever the reason, I wrote a poem about that in 2005, well into my MCC term in the Philippines where I had made a career out of peace and reconciliation.

> **Reconciliation**
> He stood behind the podium
> voice projecting loud and clear
> on Sunday after Sunday
> his sermons they came to hear
>
> As the child of a pastor
> whose job it was to preach
> strange that I don't remember
> back through my memories tho I reach
>
> But one word stands out to me
> from all the words he spoke
> a message nearly lost in mists of time
> the word brought many hope

Reconciliation sounded funny
to a boy about age twelve
within the context of scripture
concept placed inactive on a shelf

By church fathers
Who power they did seek
Forgetting words of Jesus
Loving enemies you must seek

No longer deemed impossible
That word has echoed through my life
It's taken on new meaning now
As I work to overcome hate and strife

Now I try to live that word
Showing others its meaning so clear
That reconciliation is a way of life
Perfect love casts out all fear

Twenty years ago, when I started thinking about where my passion for peace work came from, I recalled this word. I concluded that the core legacy Dad passed on to me is this concept of reconciliation. It was that singular anchor point, from all the examples, words and actions he gifted me with, that has taken root and given me a vocational grounding that endures. He could preach on that concept because the community he shepherded, the tradition that shaped him, and the legacy he wanted to pass on were all grounded in an Anabaptist counterculture.

A Small Dose of Relevant Church History

Mennonites are part of the larger Anabaptist movement begun in the early 1500s in Europe during the Reformation. The Anabaptist moniker is often confused as ANTI-Baptists, as if we are against the Baptists. In this case, "ana" refers to "re" as in "rebaptizers" or adult baptizers. During the Protestant Reformation in Europe of the 16th century, three groups emerged from the church schisms:

Roman Catholics, Protestants, and Anabaptists. Anabaptists are the smallest and least-known group. Some of the faithful during this era, intent on reform, looked to Protestant reformers like John Calvin and Martin Luther and said, "your reforms of the corrupt Catholic Church don't go far enough! You are not trying to take the life and words of Jesus seriously and live them out."

Those loosely called Anabaptist looked especially at the hard words of Jesus for their guide. They saw that he advocated allegiance to God alone, called for loving neighbors and enemies alike, and made a personal commitment to this path.

Anabaptist piety was in radical opposition to both Catholic and Protestant control through the European city state structure. Church leaders were the city governors, and city governance was the church responsibility. These leaders claimed authority over all things spiritual and material. "Kings were popes and popes were kings," a professor of mine in college emphasized. These civic leaders demanded infant baptism to register citizens to ensure state control of the population. In times of war, the church/state taxed for the war chest and conscripted citizens to fight. To rebaptize adults, as a statement of allegiance to God alone, was both heresy and sedition.

When the Ottoman Empire invaded Europe during the Reformation, the state/church leaders raised armies to protect their authority. Anabaptists, out of allegiance to God's redeeming love of all persons, refused military service and refused to fight the Turks. Branded heretics by the church, Anabaptists were hunted and killed by the state. They were tortured to recant their beliefs, but most refused and were burned at the stake, drowned, or beheaded.

This persecution scattered the budding Anabaptist movement all over Europe and drove it underground. One place where this Radical Reformation took root was Holland. A Roman Catholic Priest named Menno Simons left his Benedictine order, adopting Anabaptist beliefs. His followers were dubbed "Mennonites."

Anabaptists, hunted in Europe for their radical faith, finally tired of fleeing and sought sanctuary in the new world. My ancestors were part of the European migrant wave in the early 1700s.

Settling in a tract of land deeded by William Penn himself, they stayed on in the heart of Pennsylvania Dutch country. The cultural sand in their shoes, brought from the German low country to the rich Pennsylvania farmland, remains to this day. From the Swiss, German, and Dutch homes they left, the culture lives on in foods like sauerkraut, apple schnitz, shoofly pies, pon haus, moon pies, and bean soup.

With Pennsylvania having been founded by a Quaker espousing the nonviolence of Jesus, they found new soil where they planted, harvested, and raised families unharried.

A strange and somewhat awkward name, that: Mennonites. We are often confused with Mormons, Moravians, and Midianites. Our core identifying features are to attempt the wildly unpatriotic ideas of Jesus to extend radical mutual aid to anyone in need, love of enemies, and refusal to kill in service to country. In all of America's wars Mennonites have refused to fight. In the twentieth century, Mennonites pressed the US government for permission to do alternative service to the country in civilian and non-combatant roles as conscientious objectors.

The Mennonites of today vary in regard to how they look, theological expression, and location. I am sometimes asked, when identifying myself as Mennonite, if I drive a horse and buggy. Generally speaking, those are the Amish, our spiritual cousins. The largest Mennonite churches today are in India, Indonesia, and Ethiopia.

Mennonite Upbringing and My Dose of Cynicism

For the first years of my life, I lived in a little church bubble, spending time as a pastor's kid with people who all thought they thought alike. In retrospect, though, I now know they all *pretended* to think alike for the sake of conformity or some other motivation like fear. Sometimes external conformity breeds violence directed inward. And I experienced that as a kid.

Being incessantly heckled as a PK —preachers' kid— kept me shy and disengaged. It also kept other kids at arm's length. Church culture embedded the thought in every congregant that my dad was something other, something special. I could never live up to community expectations of being a "good boy."

The bondage placed on my psyche by having a preacher father was heavy. My friend's mother once asked me if it was okay to go fishing on a Sunday. This question has perplexed me for years. As if fishing fell on the side of work rather than play, a strict commandment to not toil on the Sabbath. For Peter, James and John maybe, but for Jon in the 1970s . . . really?

Most of what I thought I knew from those years of being churched, are now revealed as unimportant, if not downright violent. Like, for example, exclusion of women in leadership, rigid adherence to gender norms, or how the concept of "faith" is equated to an absolute surety and adherence to a rigid doctrine. Isn't that the polar opposite of faith? Isn't that called certainty?

Mennonites went through a period 80 years ago that took the demonstration of faith to embarrassing extremes. They abhorred buttons, shirt pockets, and feminine hair exposed to the sunlight, marking the darkest days of our heritage. How is it that the boundaries of who is in and who is out can be marked by such frivolity? Especially when the founder, Jesus (not Menno), tore down barriers to exclusion? It's a wonder that we as a denomination still exist given the folly of ecclesiastical walls generated by clergy and holier-than-thou adherents.

Mennonites during those distracted days crooned "Just as I am, without one plea..." a tune sung at tent revivals. What that so often meant was "come as you are but by next Sunday clean your shit up and be like us." One could never really be oneself but rather had to conform to some communal set of rules that stifled the person.

I remember the first time I learned the hard lesson that it was not okay to be honest in church. I was dragged, once again, to my uncle-the-Mennonite-bishop's rural church on a Sunday morning during a summer vacation visit to Pennsylvania. This was the kind of rectangular red brick building with steps up the entrance that excluded the disabled from entering. Those steps led into a small foyer that smelled of humid prayer-soaked hardwood. The basement of these buildings always had bland pastel-colored linoleum, smelled like damp cellars in your grandmother's house, and had buzzing florescent tubes, the kind that trigger migraines.

On that particular Sunday, I was bored sitting on the rigid oak benches staring at anything but the droning men in the pulpit. I looked up and was amused to see the shades on the dozen lights suspended from the steep arched ceiling. Burnished silver-grey, platter-shaped rounds with a convex center half-sphere hung there like extra-terrestrial aberrations. They looked for all the world like upside down flying saucers. I nearly burst out laughing as I thought of UFOs in church. I leaned over to share this observation with my mother and got a stern shush loaded with the overtones that communicated, "Your thoughts are unacceptable." A powerful message bracketed by religious pomp: "Independent thoughts, especially humorous, non-pious thoughts, are unwelcome in 'Gawd's' house," was the clear message. I felt emotionally stifled, as much as the repressive air of the summer heat in that un-airconditioned building.

An Organized Response to Suffering

As a child growing up in the Mennonite Church, I got another clear message from doing time in church pews. It had a more positive impact on my life. That message was that following Christ implied a life of service through the church, not the US military. Service, at that time and context in the 1960s, meant going out somewhere far away and foreign. The Sunday morning tales from missionaries coming through on furlough painted exciting and exotic pictures of people in faraway lands.

One story stood out in my memory of an outcast woman in some far-flung country. No man wanted to marry her, causing a very poor self-esteem. One day a man came and offered her family a dowry of fifteen cows, far above the going rate for a wife in that village. This boosted the woman's self-esteem, and she became beautiful in the eyes of both herself and everyone in the village. I acknowledge the problematic gender and cultural issues inherent in the story, even as it remained vivid in my memory. What impressed me then was that service was not just the brick and mortar of building schools or hospitals. Service included caring about and promoting dignity and self-respect.

At that time, I remember promising myself never to go to Africa as it seemed just too bizarre and far away. Even so, those missionary stories helped to put flesh on the reality of service. Being shaped by a faith tradition oriented toward service, I felt a deep impulse to be on the front lines where people were helping other people who were hungry, thirsty, or hurting. It was not long before I was moved by a desire to go into service and found myself preparing for it.

Over the past century, Mennonites have developed complex and sophisticated organizational responses to meeting human need. The denominational responses come in three forms: relief, development and, especially relevant to me in the past two decades, peacemaking.

In the heyday of denominational institution building, the Mennonite Central Committee made it possible for young people to commit to a few years of overseas or domestic voluntary service. I was proud that my church institutions had both the imagination and vision to enable large numbers of young people to "do" service as an alternative to national military conscription.

This service to others comes from the value of mutual aid among Mennonites. As a young man, I had ample opportunities to participate in short-term church structured service. The first was an Appalachian exposure trip where our church youth group did some repair in the impoverished hollers of America's coal country. Next was volunteering at a flash flood disaster site in Colorado.

Fast forward twenty years from those first service experiences, as a first time Christian in a Muslim majority country, the incessant and inescapable call to prayer had a profound impact on me. It brought the wounds of my religious bubble into focus. It forced me to re-examine my own adherence to the Gospel meta story of God's love and service to humanity. The muezzin was unabashed in proclaiming five times a day, from the tallest minarets, that God was, is and will, continue to be merciful and compassionate. In time the Islamic call to prayer urged me into gratitude of my own faith roots and tradition, an ongoing tradition that valued serving others.

Embracing My Inherited Values

To understand how the cultural pressure for Mennonite service became the vehicle for my escape to other cultures, I need to look directly to my post high school choices. In 1978, I had just graduated from Eastern Mennonite High School in Virginia. After a few months of aimless wandering, trying to figure out what to do next in life, I landed at DeVry Institute of Technology in Phoenix to study electronics.

Dropped off in a large city at the tender age of seventeen, I was overwhelmed with the details of big city living. On my own, I was both scared, yet invigorated to find my own path. The first thing I shed was my Mennonite heritage. I needed to explore other Christian traditions in order to find a faith that was workable for me. I could not just practice the belief set that was handed to me.

Historically, due to persecution, US Mennonites of European origin had a self-imposed alienation from American culture. This distance from mainstream society fostered a kneejerk reaction to reject everything "worldly:" pop culture, US judicial systems, and even participation in statecraft through something so simple as voting. That cloistered attitude meant that in every encounter with "those not us," a kind of reflexive judgment and comparison was required. So many things were forbidden, if not explicitly, then implicitly. Smoking, drinking, dancing, buttons, shirt pockets, gambling, suing damages in court, even voting. While many of those externalities of faith were jettisoned before I was born, they still held me in a mental straitjacket.

Rejecting the inherent negativity I experienced in much of my Mennonite upbringing, I struck out to find something better. I wanted a new religious tradition that would support the small, scared part of myself as I expanded to live on my own in the big bad world. I was looking for the positive side of belief.

Is it the Holy Rollers?

I stumbled upon a Pentecostal church situated right beside a major highway in Phoenix. Night after night I went to this church to have the noise and excitement of the faithful beat into my ears. I thought maybe the motion, emotion, and physicality of the Pentecostals would provide the rock I needed.

A major part of the service was the healing of sicknesses, casting out of demons, and righting all manner of ills that people brought with them to church. I observed the healing ritual numerous times until the pattern was clear to me. The preacher, in a loud and forceful voice, would shout "Be healed in the name of Jesus," pressing his hands against the victim's forehead. The person requesting healing was, at that point, "slain in the spirit." They would fall backward into the arms of the elders, who caught them and laid them on the floor, presumably, to let the magic of healing soak in.

One night I was suffering from a migraine, and I was desperate to rid myself of these headaches. So during the time of healing, I went forward to have hands laid on me. As the preacher pushed on my forehead, I was aware of his expectation that I was to fall backwards. I thought "I ain't gonna do that because I don't feel slain." He pushed harder and I resisted harder thinking, "If I'm gonna be slain, slay me and knock me out. I just won't feign this is happening." He applied a more vigorous push, my resistance rising to meet the pressure. It was then I knew, for me at least, this method was a sham, and I was not going to pretend. Faith is too serious to fake it. In the end, I never went back to the Pentecostal church. The migraines persisted.

Is it the Baptists and Their Civil Religion?

Still on my quest for belonging, I was attracted to the glitz, wealth, and energy of the North Phoenix Baptist Church. They had a video department where I was interested in the glamour of TV production. I began to attend this church that was so large it looked like a shopping mall. I devoutly attended services every Sunday morning, sometimes in the evenings, and at other special times since I didn't have much of a social life.

At every service there was an "altar call." These harangues were centered around the narrative that God is angry and would send us all to hell if we did not recite the four spiritual laws in correct order and verbiage. The altar call seemed to go on and on.

Guilt and uncertainty are powerful things and finally broke my obstinacy. One evening I went forward even though I had made a couple of commitments to Jesus in my younger years resulting in my baptism as a teen. The elder I met up at the front of the church carefully had me recite those spiritual laws. It felt to me like he was not interested in my previous commitment and church affiliation. He was only concerned with my reciting the canned salvation script. I was pressured to be immersed in the baptism pool, as the sprinkling I received in the Mennonite Church didn't seem to count. I was dunked at the front of the church a week later. Strange how, even as a card-carrying Southern Baptist, the guilt plagued me through each subsequent altar call.

The final nail in the Baptist coffin came one evening when I took my father, visiting for the weekend, to a church service. The preacher declared that in World War II, "We prayed for our boys" and were victorious. My dad, when I asked what he thought of the worship experience, gave a lukewarm response about not agreeing with everything said. That was enough for me to quit the Baptists since I too had doubts about how small a God would have to be to only bring *our* boys home from war. My immediate question was what of the prayers for the boys on the other side? Does God only listen to us with a correct salvation syntax? This all did not square.

Nope, it is the Place I Started From

Disillusioned with the previous two church experiences, I eventually chose to give one of the few Anabaptist churches in Phoenix a try. In 1979 I walked in the door of Sunny Slope Mennonite Church on a Sunday morning and immediately found that I had come home. The friendly familiarity of these folks and their outlook on life once and for all proved to me that they were my spiritual clan and the place where I belonged. In retrospect, it was a necessary journey of discovery through the Pentecostal and Baptist traditions.

The social relevance I did not find in those other Christian traditions was baked into the Mennonite value set. The experience of church shopping forced me to examine the multiplicity of my own identity. By coming back home to my religious clan, I had widened my world to understand the perspectives of other faith communities. It was a small but important step in my longer-term work at inter-religious bridge-building.

A Pop Song on the High Seas

The electronics training I had gotten right out of high school at DeVry Institute of Technology in Phoenix enabled me to get a job on an oil exploration ship.

It was September 1980, and I had just turned nineteen. We were three days out of Dutch Harbor in Alaska on a tiny tin can of a ship named the *Anne Bravo*. I had signed on to the oil exploration vessel a few weeks before. I hurried to pack and fly from Houston to the island of Unalaska, out on the Aleutian Chain. I joined the boat as it came in for a short port call to load up on fuel and supplies.

As soon as we left the shelter of the old WWII submarine base and fishing village, we hit fifteen-foot seas. Our tiny 200-foot converted coastal freighter was tossed about with ferocity. The room reared up only to be slammed down moments later in an unsyncopated jar. This wholly unnatural domain I was to call

14

home for three-week stretches shuddered as it ploughed into the trough of waves whipped high by the ferocity of the wind. Dark water crashed over the bow, adding to the violence of the ship's movement, compounding a growing sense of loneliness. We were thirty-two individual men bound together in a steel hull with a job to do, on an eternally troubled ocean.

Not yet having grasped my sense of place aboard, I was not sure where to hang out in the two-day transit to our work location, a dot on the map in the middle of the Bering Sea. Off shift from my navigation job, I sought company in the ship's day room, where off-duty crew played cards, watched TV, or just smoked cigars. Feeling like I was at the end of the world, I became nauseated by a combination of smoke, dim lights, and constant seesawing through the arctic rollers.

Someone had music on as I sat there, a bit homesick, 800 miles from land. It was a favorite hit from my adolescence, Don McClean's "American Pie." It was released in 1971, and it was at the top of the radio charts for weeks during the waning years of the American/Vietnam war. Nearly a decade later, this song still echoed with a combination of internal teenage hormonal baggage as well as external social, political, and anti-war strife. "American Pie" is a song about loss, grief, and change.

And that song, during my own self-imposed isolation from family and friends, far out to sea, expressed an anguish I could identify with at that moment. Four lines of the song jumped out. McClean croons his admiration for the Holy Trinity even as they abandon him on the day the music dies.

McClean was expressing a deep sense of abandonment I resonated with at that moment. Yet where he sang of abandonment, I felt hope. There, in that enclosed space in the forward quarters of that tiny boat, tossed about in the middle of a drenched nowhere, the Father, Son and Holy Ghost were present, even if only in the naming of their absence. No matter how abandoned McClean felt, I received comfort that night through the sung words of that pop tune.

It was clear that kind of work was not going to give me the satisfaction and happiness I sought. It was tedious work with little contact with friends and family.

However, working 80 hours a week for a year on the ship gave me enough money to head off to restart post-high school education, working toward a bachelor's degree.

The Allure of Travel

The wanderlust of exotic places I had experienced while working on the ship drew me to Goshen College in Northern Indiana because of a mandatory study-abroad component in order to graduate. I jumped into learning with abandonment and signed up for the most exotic location possible: China! This obscure little liberal arts college had the notoriety of having the first undergraduate study abroad program between the US and China just as the Middle Kingdom was opening its doors to the West in the early 1980s.

I went to China in 1983, a time in China's history and cultural development that was also a transitional nexus. Having endured the devastating Great Leap Forward and the violent Cultural Revolution, the veneration to Mao was waning fast.

Yet, when we arrived in Beijing, Chairman Mao's, huge picture, larger than life, still looked down on the dizzying stream of bicycles weaving their way in front of the Forbidden Palace. Most people wore the austere, foreboding blue or 1950s military green straight cut Mao jackets. The population was overwhelmingly rural, and most trains still ran on coal. Yet the country was beginning to feel the whiplash from accelerated modernization. Education was producing scholars to study in the West. Industry was shifting toward high tech. And urban manufacturing demanded a flood of rural to urban migration. To be a witness to that, as one of the few Westerners present in the country at the time, was an intoxicating thing.

I was to teach English to college students our own age. On the one hand, inept as a teacher, I grasped for anything that might aid in teaching a class full of eager Chinese college students.

Sheepishly, I have to admit I introduced the Oscar Meyer Wiener advertising jingle to talk about US pop culture. When not teaching, our days were full of cultural field trips visiting monasteries, learning ancient Chinese history and Daoism, and seeing panda bears in the zoo.

If you had known me in China as a study-abroad student, you might have wagered I would never again set foot out of the USA. I was maladjusted, complained a lot, and regularly pined for home. I chafed at the restrictions put on our group by the Chinese authorities. I railed at the bugs that took up residence in my gut and made me inhabit the commode for extended periods.

In reflection years later, my maladjustment in China was an indication that I was only surviving and not thriving with each move I made as a child. That mobility had not given me the gift of adaptability, but rather I coped through withdrawal and numbness. Now, shouldering the full responsibility of my own choices to step into a new place, I was intensely uncomfortable.

Despite my discomfort, something in me came alive while standing on the nexus of cultures. While I got the night soil on my shoes from gardens surrounding the campus where we were housed, China was not a place I longed to return. I was, however, convinced that living and serving outside my own country was a competency I had not yet mastered but wanted to. I was drawn to experiencing life as an outsider. I caught a vision of being someone who stood as a bridge between worlds.

This study abroad experience in China exhausted the small pile of cash I had earned working on a ship. I suspended my college studies for a few years, got married, and supported Carolyn until she graduated from Goshen College in 1985.

2

Partners

"PULL OVER," SHE COMMANDED, "I need out."

I swung our dull gray '75 Vega Kammback off the westbound lane of Highway 160 with a swirl of dust. We were cresting La Veta Pass in southern Colorado when I skidded the car to a stop by the green highway sign boldly proclaiming the summit 9,413 feet above sea level.

The alpine hills that made up the top of the pass were dry from southern sun exposure. The stunted evergreen trees standing sentinel at timberline contrasted to the deep blue of the sky. Brilliant yellow-white clouds held infinite shades of gray within their billowy shadows. The aromatic respiration of wind-gnarled pine trees tainted the cool, thin air with a scent that still held the frigidity of last season's snow. The crumbling sandstone shoulder made for a hardscrabble respite from driving cross-country.

On that crisp morning, the beauty of our surroundings did nothing to cool down our heated conversation. Carolyn's pleading tone held a hot edge.

"What you wanna do doesn't make sense considering our longer-term goal," she argued. "I need a job. I feel like a noose is around my neck from the burden of these loans," she pled. "Can we really take off for three years of volunteer work with this debt?"

"You can get a job anywhere, and I want to go back to the Pacific Northwest," I countered. "You know I fell in love with that wild country before we met. I want to look for a program there and finish my degree before we go."

"Why make this so hard? We don't know anybody in Alaska, and wouldn't it be better to be close to family so they can help in our transitions?" she stated with exasperation.

I mulled this over as we sat apart for a few minutes, getting space from the intensity of the argument.

Carolyn and I had been married less than a year before, August 1984, and this was our most severe conflict to date, frightening both of us by its intensity. For a conflict avoider by nature, this was unfamiliar territory for me because we were trapped in the car on a cross country trip together.

I had always fled conflict when I could. As a middle child, sibling conflict was usually between an older sister and younger brother with me being the mediator in between their spats. My ego crumbled when conflict was directed at me.

Having just graduated from a nursing program, Carolyn held the ticket to the wider world. She was highly employable, and I counted on her income while I finished my undergraduate studies as I had just done when she finished her nursing degree. Yet she was feeling the weight of her school loans and pressure to land a job somewhere soon.

What we had decided as a medium-term plan for the next few years involved a more serious upheaval. We were both committed to an international volunteer term with the Mennonite Central Committee, but I wanted to finish my college degree before then. It would only take me a few years since I already had three years of post-high school credits on my transcripts. So, the location where I finished my undergrad education would only be a temporary, short-term waypoint at best. It would have to be a place where we would not get too attached, given our goals of volunteer service. The decision had to be made as quickly as possible. It was already early summer.

"You do have a point," I finally conceded. "But it's Alaska!" I cried, "Doesn't that excite you, intrigue you just a bit?"

She refuted, "You know the energy it will take…the money… and you know how both are in such short supply right now. We don't know anybody there and we'll have no help making that move," she stated flatly.

And with that final argument, I conceded.

The She of Us

Carolyn, my senior by twenty months, comes from a hardworking, close-knit farm family of seven. As the middle child of five siblings, she learned to defer her wishes to more vocal older sisters and the expectations placed on her younger brothers. The poultry farm she grew up on, however, got the bulk of familial attention. She attended the same school with her peers all the way from kindergarten to high school. She had rarely ventured out of the state in those formative years.

At first deferring her vocational calling for fear of mastery over the hard sciences, she finally gathered the self-assurance to return to school and complete her bachelor of science in nursing. Carolyn exudes a confident balance between her professional life and the maternal instincts and the domestic skills that she gleaned from her mother. She is a creative baker, naturally experimental cook, and practical homemaker. I was attracted to her as an anchor in my life. Juxtaposed to my transient childhood, Carolyn is rooted in an actual, physical place in her understanding of home.

Carolyn's quiet demeanor caught my eye when I first met her. I was immediately attracted to her simple, yet elegant style, which quietly asserts her rock stable self-assurance. Upon first sight, I noticed a twinkle in her beautiful blue eyes. I filed that image of her face away in the "gotta get to know you better" folder of my brain. We did indeed get to develop a friendship when we both attended Goshen College in northern Indiana. We had our first date on a cold winter's night, opting to see a movie on campus. I walked her to her apartment, kissed her, and the flame ignited. As our relationship burned hotter, infatuation cooked into something more durable: companionship.

With a stable profession as a nurse, I mused upon first meeting her, Carolyn could easily be the breadwinner since I still had no clue what I wanted to be when I grew up.

The Me of Us

In my mid-twenties, I was a wiry, thin man who stooped forward ever so slightly as if my full shaggy beard pulled me off balance. Not quite six feet, I had solid, muscular legs and skinny arms from years of biking. My vision was corrected since grade school with one eye weaker than the other requiring one lens being twice as thick. By the time I met Carolyn, I had already known the scarce times of minimum wage jobs and making ends meet as a bachelor. Thanks to my predisposition as a practical, do-it-yourself kind of guy, my life was held together with duct tape in a literal and metaphorical sense. In college, I could be seen wearing the same, checkered flannel shirt for several days in a row. "Why should I wash something that", sniff sniff, "doesn't smell?" I would say as I lifted an arm checking the validity of that statement.

At Goshen College, where we met, there was a lecturer I admired. Gathering up the courage to have coffee with this professor, I picked his brain for vocational advice. With a snort, he renounced academics who were so narrowly focused on their own field they lacked common sense. "I know some who can't change the tire on their own car," he scoffed. "Being a generalist," he continued, "is a worthy calling in this age of hyper specialization." I took him to heart and set about learning a little bit about a great many things. In doing so, I also developed the powers of observation. The connectedness of all things revealed themselves to me as the pattern of the universe.

The downside of being a generalist is that I have a hard time committing to anything. I bounce around from job to job, never satisfied with what I am doing. I am always wishing to be somewhere else, in another job or pining for other skills than the ones I am currently employing. The genesis of my lack of commitment comes, in part, from my parents' mobility during my formational years. Perhaps attention to the next move kept them from focusing on me as a middle kid who fell between the cracks. Their lack of encouragement to become something . . . firefighter, pilot, welder . . . translated into a message of ambiguity about deciding what I wanted to be when I grew up. When it came time for a career, I did not really have career aspirations, just a series of jobs I had mostly hated.

It was at Goshen College that I had my first off-continent experience. The Peoples Republic of China had recently opened its doors to the West. The college president, having sustained some significant relationships in China through the closed years, had developed the first undergraduate exchange program between the US and China. I signed up and went with a group in the fall of 1983. My study abroad experience in the Middle Kingdom convinced me that I wanted to spend my days navigating the world's cornucopia of cultures.

Yet that separation from Carolyn made being in China difficult. While we had only been dating six months before I left for China, the intensity to develop a shared life together was so great that I wrote letters to her every day. Half my brain was still with Carolyn in Goshen.

Us

Carolyn and I had been on our own several years, and we were both older students. We were ready soul mates. Our relationship blossomed rapidly as we discussed life and values and family on those first few late-night cups of coffee in the college snack shop. We became best friends, and it was a natural and fairly undramatic decision to get married.

In my bombastic, shock and awe kind of way, I declared I wanted to get married in a hot air balloon, in part to limit the number of guests and the pomp of the whole affair. I disliked weddings, the expectations, anxiety of planning, and the dress-up fakeness. In the end we married in Colorado at 9,600 feet. On the massif of Pikes Peak, our venue was a small summer camp tucked between steep aspen-covered hills. The location was perfect for a simple wedding and, ironically, a higher altitude than a hot air balloon would have been. The compact A-frame chapel overlooked a small pond and beyond to the steep sides of a montane hillside affectionately called Monkey Rock. The camp, a mile and half up a steep single lane path, had enough beds to billet all of our fifty-three guests. Being remote, only a small group attended including Carolyn and my family, friends, and our parental invitees.

The day before the ceremony, we conscripted our family and a few guests to clean the fly specks off the chapel windows that nearly occluded the rugged view of Monkey Rock across the alpine ravine. Compensation for this labor came in the form of my brother's famous grilled chicken cookout as the setting sun plunged the valley into early evening's shadow. Guests retired to their rustic cabins or camping tents.

It was an uncomplicated wedding to match our commitment to a simple, practical lifestyle. Carolyn's dress, her sister's handiwork, was completed the day before the wedding. I wore white linen pants and a tropical-style white shirt. Our flowers were wildflowers from the riot of color found in the high plain's ditches of Eastern Colorado. Reception cuisine was equally basic: Mom baked a chocolate sheet cake with green mint icing to go with cold cuts and veggies.

We said the vows we wrote ourselves We then hiked across from the small valley and up a short rock-strewn path to a multistory chalet aptly named Emmental after its namesake in the Swiss Alps. The view from the balcony was stunning: Pikes Peak and the clearly delineated tree line on the ridge 3,000 feet below it.

After celebrating with our guests, we escaped to our highly decorated car. Dogged by revelers halfway down the twisting gravel road to the highway, we finally were on our own. Our first wedding night turned out to be a $50/night motel in Cripple Creek with a tiny tin shower insert.

The wedding probably cost less than $1000 with all the volunteer work, simple decorations, and natural beauty we used in the location. It fitted our collective sense of responsibility to tread lightly on the planet.

Flash forward to our argument on the crest of La Veta Pass. We stuck with the tensions, talked them out, and found resolution as we always have in our marriage. By the end of the drive back east, we knew what to do. A few phone calls netted a job for Carolyn and a school placement for me. We would keep driving east and stop, for a few years, on the prairies of central Kansas so I could finish my undergraduate work. In the fall of 1985, we landed temporarily in North Newton, home to Bethel College.

3

Preparing For Service

A Stopover in Kansas

The tiny borough of North Newton is where we would reside for only fifteen months. The north side of town peters out into the vast plains of central Kansas. The college was like a gateway into town going south or the open skies and fields to the north.

Home, for that short stopover, was a small one-room apartment above a garage on a quiet street within walking distance of the college. Before the fad of tiny houses, this compact 400 square feet included a narrow kitchen tucked in the front-side dormer. We were limited to standing full height only in the center of the small living room due to the steeply sloping roofline. That first winter was brutal. Partly due to limited finances driving our frugality, we opted not to run the baseboard electric heating. Instead, we huddled on the floor around a plug-in space heater in the mornings when the room temperature dipped into the low 40s. The attic apartment had no insulation in the floor so the drafty open garage door would freeze the carpet in our living room. It was so cold in that apartment during the subzero dead of winter that the neighboring apartment's pipes froze because we kept our side so cold.

Bethel College, a small Mennonite institute for higher learning, had a unique program that attracted my attention. International development, a recently introduced course of study, seemed a perfect fit for me with my newfound desire for exploring life outside the US. I wanted my work domain to be global with a focus on poverty alleviation and mitigating the suffering from impacts of war.

The goal of the international development program was to prepare students to work at uplifting the poor and marginalized around the world. I grew to understand how patronizing and neocolonial that attitude could be. Development, implemented as an arm of foreign policy, forced those being "developed" to accede to US imperialism.

In all fairness to Bethel's program, students were urged to listen to and respect local wisdom while honoring the dignity and agency of each person. This mentality was already baked into the Mennonite in me.

International agriculture was one of the required courses I needed for degree completion. For the practical part of the agriculture study, students left the classroom to tend an actual garden containing real soil and plants. So, I waded into the chigger-infested plot near the school to learn a thing or two about gardening and her big brother agriculture. The conditions in arid central Kansas mirrored many places in sub-Saharan Africa where graduates of the international development program might end up working. I threw myself into this course knowing it may soon be relevant.

While the instructors incorporated all the state-of-the-art sustainable agriculture practices known in that day, what intrigued me the most was making a compost pile. The art of composting is the practice of growing soil. Mixing the discarded peels of vegetables and fruits as well as grass clippings, leaves, and tree trimmings to regenerate worn out soil was, it seemed to me, the ultimate recycling process. All that plant and bio matter was part of a circular system of which vegetables are a byproduct. This greatly appealed to the practical, frugal, and bohemian side of me.

I learned that compost needs a few ingredients to work well. Those include green matter providing the nitrogen — fresh grass clippings work well — and brown matter providing the carbon — leaves, cornstalks, sawdust, etc. To get the digestion of the carbon and nitrogen going, add a source of microbes — either rich soil or manure of some kind. The right amount of moisture and air combined with the right conditions encourage the microbes to break down the other matter, creating an enormous amount of heat. The resulting compost binds and regenerates worn out soil, enhancing both soil cohesiveness and its ability to hold moisture. Healthy soil breaks down through the abuse of mono-cropping, soil compaction from heavy tractors driving over the fields, and loss of ground cover. Runoff from heavy rains further depletes the soil. Compost reverses these traumas.

Conflict Composting

Another course required at Bethel College was a peace-related course. The parlance of conflict transformation was just beginning to be understood within academic circles. Conflict transformation is reframing conflict as a neutral, raw energy that can be used for improved relationships and enhanced trust among other, more technical understandings. Truth be told, I have always had discomfort with the term *conflict transformation* because it is so nondescript and sterile.

It's in my nature to see connections everywhere, so blending concepts of peace and gardening came naturally to me. Composting has stuck with me all these years as a metaphor for transforming the pain and suffering of violence. *Composting* is a much more organic metaphor than *transformation* because it intrinsically includes the processes of life, death, and regeneration. Conflict composting reframes the wounds of violence as a resource with which to compost (transform) conflict into something restorative.

To start conflict composting, we will look at the so-called rubbish that destructive conflict can leave in its wake. Individual or community experience with violent conflict leaves trauma, disconnection, fear, and mistrust among other things. People often see these impacts as bad and wish to get over them as quickly as possible with pat phrases like "moving on" and "turning a new page." In a post-war context, the litter of brokenness is often covered up like so much garbage in a landfill and the open wounds and scars are actively kept out of sight.

Air and water are but two elements of four — earth, air/sky, water, fire — that are sacred to indigenous spiritualities and necessary to all life on earth. Air and water should not be owned by any individual but freely available to all. Air corresponds to the rich tapestry of communications within our relationships. Communicating with those around us happens by pheromone, body language, emotion, and, oh yes, voice. While violence alienates, healthy, respectful communication reconnects. If air is analogous to communication, then too little of that element will leave us with unresolved and/or uncomposted residuals from damaging conflict.

The right amount of water is crucial for microbe health and makes our compost bind together. In conflict composting, this is analogous to our bonds of clan or tribe. Understanding our valued place within the more complex social structures surrounding us binds us to that community in healing ways through rights, obligations, and responsibilities.

Cut off from those elements, we are quickly incapacitated by isolation and eventually cease developing just as our soil composting process would stop. When we tend to a balance of these two elements, air/communications and water/tribe, the result is a thriving conflict composting process.

The microscopic miracles called microbes turn a pile of stinking manure and rotting vegetable matter into life-giving soil. Microbes are analogous in our conflict composting to the spiritual miracles of life that turn our piles of painful memory into something that improves our lives and others. The energy that moves the soul to forgiveness, healing and restoration (transformation)is somewhat of a mystery, but we know its work by the results. Time is the ally of the microbes, the mystery of composting, and thus we have hope because we see it is possible to transcend the present stinky mess we have been given.

In my life of peacebuilding work, I have seen many who, having gone through the fire of violence, trauma, or loss, bloom into rich inspiration. I have also met many people who have been toxified by their cultures and systems. Conflict composting is understanding that conflict produces some intense byproducts that accumulate over the years. Brokenness, mistrust, trauma, wounds, and a gradual hardening of the heart all can result if we do not transform conflict into healing, trust, wholeness, and love. The cohesion of community has been broken by the heavy machinery of war. It's time to gather these cast-off elements to grow some healthy vegetables of peace.

And so, I completed my bachelor's degree between the fall of 1985 and the winter of 1986. Those short three semesters of studying international development and peace gave me a way of observing and processing the foreign and exotic world Carolyn and I were about to encounter.

Applying to Volunteer

While I was finishing my bachelor's degree, we applied to the Mennonite Central Committee (MCC) for a volunteer assignment. Once we had completed the necessary application and paperwork, they offered us a position in Central Africa. The decision where to go had an ironic twist.

"Did you read the reports that accompanied the job description for the position in Chad?" I queried Carolyn.

"Yeah, I didn't like what I read. Those volunteers lost all their pictures when their pickup truck got hijacked at gunpoint," she responded. "They could have been killed!"

"But they weren't," I refuted lamely. "Besides, in Chad we could learn French and that would be a plus on our resumes."

"I don't want to go there," she stated flatly. "Let's ask MCC to if there is another placement in Africa somewhere."

So we did. Out of the fire and into the frying pan. We were accepted as volunteers to a refugee support project, living in a refugee camp in Northwest Somalia. Carolyn was to work with maternal/child health. I was assigned to help equip refugees for life beyond the camp, learning technical skills that were portable for when they returned home.

We had settled on Somalia by my last semester at Bethel College. I was able to research the political, social, and economic realities of our new location. It was the first time in my life I had the luxury of such extensive preparation for the next place I was to live.

I moved often as a child. I was in a different school for the first five years of my schooling career. By the time I graduated from college I needed two hands and two feet to tally the places I lived. By this point in my life, I was a nomad.

So, it seemed fitting that Carolyn and I ended up working in a place in the world that was geographically suited to nomadic life, the Horn of Africa, specifically, Somalia. But the realities of the region tempered my wanderlust.

From gardening and composting to analyzing conflict, international development and relief aid, Bethel College prepared me to think about the new contexts and cultures as I entered them. With renewed commitment to Mennonite values of service and endowed with a newly minted bachelor's degree in international development, I charged off to change the world.

4

Land of Rocks and Sand and Camels

Change

greet the change
  as the morning dew
    something that wets the feet
      and sparkles with iridescence
        to delight the eyes
          until the morning sun
            with its persistent heat
            and ageless arc
            burns it away by noon
          and we are left
          with bittersweet memory
          anticipating its return
        at the next crossing
      of day to night
    and night to day

The First Day

At the tender age of twenty-six, I arrived in Mogadishu that first
day in January 1987 on a battered old Boeing 707. A blast of

sodden tropical heat greeted Carolyn and me when the plane door swung open over the tarmac.

I enthusiastically stepped out onto the aircraft stairs to a vista that overwhelmed my senses. I squinted at the deep azure blue of the Indian Ocean and the sunbaked yellow orange sand of the beach on the far side of the runway. The fishy smell of saltwater and hot dust filled my nostrils.

As oppressive as the heat and stark view was, the bigger jolt came from the unfamiliar culture that swirled at the bottom of the air stairs. Soldiers strolled by with battered old AK-47s while blue-bereted police barked loud rapid-fire directions. Then there was the disorganized scramble across the airport ramp to the immigration shed, where passengers were "welcomed." This bureaucratic disorder signaled ominous things to come.

The volatility of Somalia I had read about doing research for my recently completed undergraduate degree was pressed home in real time. When I read analysis predicting an imminent political collapse, I was scared on the one hand and intrigued on the other. What would it be like to be in a nation disintegrating from years of authoritarian divide and rule, I wondered? I knew Somalia was a front-line state in the Cold War, so going there seemed significant somehow.

I had lofty expectations about what I could accomplish in this type of environment. That grandiose vision set by my chosen course of studies created a high bar: bring *development* to places that were *undeveloped*. My degree program had enough nuance to force me to grapple, at least intellectually, with the limitations and utility of that term *development*.

Standing on the tarmac, in a flash of clarity, it came to me that my assumptions had yet to be tested for real-world relevance, my mettle untried in times of tension. The full-frontal assault on my senses upon arrival heightened my excitement and enthusiasm at being in Somalia.

The First Night

I lay awake that first night in the sweltering tropical night air in the sand-strewn city of Mogadishu. I desperately tried to find sleep. Peaceful slumber was elusive after a day and a half of travel with an eight hours' time zone difference. My monkey mind raced, replaying the mayhem that greeted me upon arrival.

Glass shards topped walls, meant to thwart thieves, hemmed in the narrow streets of the capitol city. The whitewashed walls enclosing the compounds near upscale Villa Somalia also kept out any hint of sea breeze. The lone fan, stopping and starting with each brownout on the unstable electricity grid, had limited ability to give relief to my sweating attempt to sleep on the lumpy bed. Clawing at slumber, I was bedeviled by lingering heat radiating off block walls. The self-imposed confinement under the mosquito net draped over the bed added to my misery. The nets kept the incessant whine of mosquitoes out of direct earshot, but more importantly, staved off protozoa-laden bites transmitting malaria. Nets gave an extra layer of suffocation under the thick, stagnant night air.

My mind raced, processing the shock experienced during my arrival. It signified an innate sensitivity to the individuals and systems I engaged. My initial questions were about basic survival. "How are those poor souls able to eat? The ones in torn and dirty rags for clothes who were begging as I left the airport. Where do they sleep?"

My next questions had to do with the structural and political realities that I had read about in college. "What were those soldiers shouting about? How often do they fire their weapons? How often did the tensions break into open violence?" I wondered who was watching as my passport was stamped in at immigration.

The initial impacts of this new location pushed their way into my consciousness in a physical way I couldn't ignore. "Is it always this hot? When will the rain come? How will I ever learn Somali? How will I ever drive safely here since the road rules don't seem to apply?"

The quiet air was split with the loud crack of gunfire, jolting me to alertness. Uphill or downhill, I couldn't tell from the reverberation off block walls. The sound removed any possibility of sleep at the periphery of my travel-weary consciousness. That lone shot in the darkness, like a starter shot at the beginning of a race, signaled that I crossed a threshold. It began the dismantling of my simplistic construct of my reality. It was the first volley that set off a quest to find an inner peace in spite of the growing violent complexity in the world around me.

I have often pondered what it was about that first rifle report echoing through the streets of Mogadishu that seemed to make my world turn on its axis. What was that shift about? Why did it seem to take so very little to knock me off center?

In that moment, in the dark with all the sudden unknowns focused by that single shot, I was scared. I know that now. As I think back to that pivotal moment, I understand that my propensity for emotional responses to stressful situations also limited my bandwidth for rational, in-situ processing.

The only time I had ever heard firearms being discharged was for target practice and hunting. The power of a shotgun blast caused me, at the young age of twelve, to pause in wonderment at my own agency. I remember that dawning realization when walking with my cousin in the fields of rural Pennsylvania hunting crows. It was summer and we had little to do. A murder of crows circled lazily over the fields and alighted noisily in the trees of the fence row. My older cousin and I loaded up shotguns and started stalking silently toward the crows. I turned to him and blurted out loud how that double-barrel twelve-gauge slung over my arm gave me the power to take life!

It was a stark moment in my understanding of the world, and I took it seriously. It shaped a larger question: "What other ways do I wield power over the world?" It was a question, at that moment of mid-puberty, that was both weighty and exhilarating. That early awareness of my own impact on the world has stayed with me as a bane and blessing ever since. Bane as I understand more deeply the privilege my social status, skin color and economic access that, in my having it, marginalizes others. Blessing in that I am capable of effecting change toward greater justice.

So, when the shot was fired, echoing off the dark walls in Mogadishu, I reacted viscerally with fear. I had never before thought of gunfire as a message to another human. I had never before been so close to the space where that hostile communication took place. That single ballistic report could mean anything on a long spectrum from "I'm warning you to stay away!" to expressing enough venom and hatred to blast "I'm going to kill you!"

The sonic void that followed was deafening, as if the message of the gun was preeminent over all other sound, silencing all other voices. In my hyperactive imagination, the person on the receiving end of the gun was silenced and may lay dying in the street.

In some ways my naivete saved me a lot of angst by not knowing all that could go wrong, all that could hurt me. The dangers in Somalia were myriad and could come out of nowhere. The protozoa responsible for giardia. Road accidents. Crocodiles and hippos in the river. Or the roof falling in. Yes, there was a time when I heard a huge *crash* in the MCC guest house next door. I ran over to the other side of the duplex to discover a huge chunk of the poured slab roof had come loose from the ceiling's rusty rebar and fell the ten feet to smash flat the kitchen table in the representatives' side of the house.

The unpredictability and chaos would continue to dismantle my outer resolve to do good and increase an inner disquiet to a loud cacophony.

5

Urban Adjustments

Morning Soundscape

Dawn's urban music
All faithful arise for prayer
Allah al Akbar

Urban

Those first days in the country were overwhelming enough without concerning myself with risk from underlying conflict, structural injustice, and clan dynamics that would ultimately lead to Somalia's total collapse. The effort needed for cross-cultural adjustment threatened to swamp me as the information moved from cerebral to sensory. My senses were in overdrive as I took in all that surrounded me.

Somalia was so unlike anything I had experienced to that point in life. The rural landscape just at the south end of the runway and the urban sprawl at the north end of the airport evidenced, from a first approximation, huge disparities and differences.

Our first days were in the urban environment of the capitol city Mogadishu. A sprawling city with hints of its Italian Colonial past, "Mog" as we called it, was situated on the sand-swept dunes looking east, out over the expansive Indian Ocean.

Even with the second longest coastline on the African continent, most Somalis oriented themselves toward the interior bush land rather than marine life. Perhaps it was deep affinity with herding animals in the sparsely populated bush lands and the pastoral life that led Somalis to turn inland away from the vast open water. Nomadic sensibilities dictated the organization of their towns and urban centers.

The first weeks Carolyn and I spent in orientation were mostly in Mogadishu. My senses were often overloaded by all that was new during that honeymoon phase of adjustment. With the physical stress of the heat, noise, and mental acclimation, I often needed an afternoon nap. I grew to understand why taking siesta in the tropics is a matter of prudent survival more than a luxury.

Carolyn, in one of her first letters to her parents, described excitement and intrigue, arriving at our new home in Somalia.

> There is so much new. I am bubbling with excitement in this phase of culture shock . . . a real sense of "everything is great" type attitude. I'm going to enjoy it while it lasts.
> — 19 January 1987

Hearing

On that first morning, I was jolted awake by the universal test of a live PA system, "fww pffww pwfffww" of breath into the microphone. It was immediately followed by the *Allah Al Akbar*, but in the flourish of this particular muezzin, it sounded more like *Waallah wal Wakbar*, the "a" taking on a deeper resonance of meaning and purpose by articulating the open mouth, rounder and fuller, as if to dredge the depths of the meaning of God.

Islam requires the faithful to pray regularly beginning with a call to prayer before sunrise. Right next to the compound where I had finally drifted into a fitful sleep, the mosque's loudspeakers boomed the urgent invocation to pray.

Starting in the early morning hours before dawn from then on, I was greeted with the city erupting with calling the faithful to pray. *Allah al Akbar* — God is great — would follow that initial broken stillness.

It is a singular call, in hundreds of mosques in thousands of cities in the hearts of a billion plus believers around the world. It is a declared and practiced faith five times a day. The soundscape is punctuated by muezzins on a spectrum of pleasantly melodious to off-key tone deaf. Proclaiming that God is Great, God is compassionate and merciful, and that Mohammed, peace be upon him, is the Prophet of God.

The antiquity! The faithfulness! The beauty!

It was loud! It was disruptive! It felt invasive!

This five times daily interruption would often be so loud that any conversation would need to cease until the call to prayer ended. In those first days and weeks the exotic turned into irritation for me. It seemed I just couldn't escape the incessant, public prayers. Later though, it eventually blended into the soundscape. The call to prayer was just one more noise like horns honking, dogs barking, roosters crowing, and one-cylinder motorcycles putt-putting by.

The Somali language, once likened to the bark of machine gun fire, sounded foreign and strange to my ears. Peppered with Arabic and Swahili, it was written down only fifteen years before I first set foot in the country. Previous MCC volunteers had warned us not to mistake the brief time as a written language for lack of literacy. Somalis have a rich tradition of poetry and clever linguistic nuance that could pinpoint a person's speech to their region and clan. I later learned that Somalis could recite their ancestors to the tenth generation, another characteristic of this largely oral culture. Somalis also show their linguistic prowess through the ability to insult someone or their clan eloquently, hidden in poetry or prose.

In a time long before the ubiquitous mobile phones and text messages, I saw the famed "Somali bush telegraph" in action. An event that happened in northwest Somalia was relayed a few days later by someone in Eastleigh, a suburb of Nairobi, Kenya, 745 miles away! Friends told me of the Somalis who worked in the telephone exchange in the Arabian Gulf States and, on the sly, connected the diaspora to pass news. The oral culture had a force behind it that networked the latest happenings far and wide.

I count learning the Somali language as one of my greatest sources of pride. While I was not fluent in reading, at the height of my ability to speak, I never feared going anywhere without a translator. Although I do not dream anymore in Somali, the accomplishment of learning at least one other language still gives me a deep satisfaction.

One delight to my ears was the camel bell. I will never forget that distinctive hollow thud made by the camel bells. Hollowed out ovals of hardwoods with a wooden clapper or two, these bells thunked randomly as camels wandered with a dromedary's side-to-side gait through cities, towns, and the bush. Just loud enough for nomads to gauge the location and identity of each animal, they made a pleasant, earthy sound.

With time I grew to love the consistency of the morning sounds of roosters crowing, donkeys braying, and the call to prayer. Both in urban and rural settings, the world noisily wakes up with each new dawn.

Smell

Exploring the city the first days after my arrival yielded new and exotic aromas that raided my nostrils.

My nose quickly picked up the musky smell that only domesticated farm animals make. Cows and camels, tended by urban herders who had the abattoir or animal markets as their goals, shushed the animals lazily along the sandy streets and byways of the city. Free-range goats and sheep wandered the streets, untended, foraging as best they could on the scrub bushes that struggled out of the cracks in vacant lots.

I picked up another scent that wafted on the winds while walking through the town, the spicy sweet smell of aromatic tree resins. The Horn of Africa covers part of Northern Kenya, Eastern Ethiopia, present day Somalia, Somaliland and Djibouti. This area is home to trees that ooze syrupy resins that, when collected, harden into rock like nodules. Since the days of the Egyptian Pharaohs, merchants traded these valuable gums, frankincense and myrrh, throughout the region and beyond.

Water is scarce in the arid times between seasonal rains. So personal hygiene is practiced, not by frequent washing with water, but by bathing in the smoke laced with these burning resins. Red-hot charcoal is placed in a small ceramic thurible; the spice is heaped on the hot coals and the scented smoke envelopes the bather. The smell, as does a quality perfume, lingers on the wearer long into the day.

Few smells are as strongly nostalgic for me as the East African bushland hardwoods burning from a cook or campfire. The wood of North America does not smell quite the same. It's as if the smoke of burning African acacia wood releases its life force magic, drawing the smeller deep into the very soil story of the continent.

There were other, less enticing, smells. Clouds of choking diesel smoke, kerosene cookstove fuel, sewer roaches, and open sewage to name a few. When I smell these pungent odors today, I am transported decades back in time and continents away.

Taste

Carolyn and I were greeted early on with a palate of exotic tastes. The cardamom-and-clove flavored, overly sweetened milk tea, ritually served in social settings was an easy taste to acquire.

I grew to desire the acrid smoky flavor of thick, creamy camel's milk. The milk was collected in hollowed-out wooden containers, called *dhil*, which, once emptied, were upended over a wood fire for sterilization. With each milking, the smoke flavor laced the milk. We once had smoke-flavored ice cream made from this milk.

The stale, insectoid flavor of weevils became a routine "spice" infused in the bread we ate. Flour stored in warehouses on the docks for far too long, became infested with these grain-eating pests. People sifted all flour before use, yielding piles of caraway seed-shaped black bugs. Even the most meticulous sifting could not remove the tiny weevil eggs, and so the rancid flavor permeated the newly baked bread. I learned in the first week that the distinct taste of weevils, once pointed out, is impossible to forget.

The Italians had a brief flirtation with colonization in Somalia before World War II. The Somali civil service, trained in Italy, fit well into the Mediterranean atmosphere of southern Italy, which had a similar climate to coastal Mogadishu. Pasta is one enduring legacy from that era which embedded itself as the staple food of Somalis. Even though inland Somalia remained much as it had for millennia, the influence of pasta, called *basta* in Somali language, became an important food found in even the most remote location. *Basta* is often served with a heaping pile of chopped goat meat, boiled or fried. Replete with bone shards, goat has a gamy, barnyard taste. In time, I came to crave sesame oil fried goat liver and onions with fresh bread, as my preferred breakfast. Later in my Somali tenure, I sampled the tallowy sweet fat of camel hump.

Touch/Tactile

"Get Birkenstocks," urged the only slightly more seasoned volunteers who had gone before us on assignment in Africa. "They are sturdy and cool." These expensive sandals have a contoured cork insole and wide leather straps. They looked perfect for rugged, hot, tropical climates. What we did not count on was the impracticality of the bowls made by the deep insole where our feet rested. The lips surrounding our feet, acting as a scoop with each step, filled up with sand that was difficult to remove without taking the sandals off. Ninety-nine cent foam flip-flops worked better until I went on a lark in the bush. In that case, the four-inch thorns from acacia trees penetrated the thin protective foam and embedded themselves in my still tender feet. Despite their vulnerabilities, I wore that cheap footwear most of the time, going months without ever putting on a closed toe shoe.

Another tactile oddity was the greasy stain of diesel fuel, which powered all our vehicles. With perpetual fuel uncertainty at the few fuel stations around the city, we always had several drums of diesel in our compound. This necessitated pumping it into the truck with a hand pump. Inevitably some would slosh onto my hands, clothes and even one time, soaked my journal in a suitcase sitting near the drum. With running water a precious commodity everywhere in the country, washing the sticky stench of fuel off my hands was impossible.

While my senses continued to be flooded, my brain needed to process more complex concepts. Different traditions, norms and conventions took adaptation too. I had already dreaded driving with its hazards. The rules of the road were so vastly different as well.

Stoplight: Not Running From Trouble

One sweltering day in Mogadishu, I was driving down toward the old city. As it was almost noon, the traffic was particularly bad, and peoples' patience had just about run out for the day. With so many non-functioning stoplights in the city, I had developed an unfortunate driving reflex of ignoring them and shot thru the intersection based on an opening in traffic, ignoring the red light. As I turned the corner, a policeman was standing there. He waved me over. It was only at that point that I looked to see the light was working.

I could see the glint in this policeman's eye . . . *ahhh a big take . . . a foreigner who broke our traffic laws.* He must have figured I was worth at least 1000 shillings in "baksheesh," or "money for tea" as bribes were euphemistically known.

It was part of the traffic game in Somalia to pay as little to the police as possible when getting pulled over. *No one* ever goes to the police station to pay the fine. The infraction is just settled on the street between those unfortunate enough to be pulled over and the man in uniform.

That day I was feeling very adventurous with unexamined privilege. I decided that I *wanted* to visit the police station to pay my fine just to see what would happen.

After convincing the traffic cop that I indeed wanted to go to the city police station because I had broken the law, we went.

The sergeant handling the traffic violations for the day was a seasoned old Italian trained civil servant. He listened as my translator pled my case and then to the police officer recount my offence against the laws of the land.

The sergeant asked me if I knew the fine for running the light, and I said, "yes, 3000 shillings." Then the sergeant said "Okay, 200 shillings because Somalia and USA are friends." I figured I got a bargain since the experience was worth at least 500 shillings.

6

Rural Resilience

Tree Song

Acacia trees sing
wind whistles through pin sharp thorns
green songs come with rain

I was fortunate to spend time out in the semi-arid wilds of Somalia. I was intoxicated with the raw, sensual overload and overwhelming beauty of these sub-Saharan nomadic range lands. My observations during this time in my life served to shape an increased sensitivity to the natural world.

Somalia in the 1980s was exotic in that so few Westerners had ever ventured there. It was mostly rural with a harsh, arid climate. Nomads herded their camels, goats and sheep, roaming from well to well, grazing area to grazing area. Following the explosion of green that came with the rains, herding animals in the bush was the way of life for a majority of people in the country.

There is a tree native to East Africa I called *acacia*. Scientifically, I do not know much about the tree or even how many species there are in the region. I did observe that this flat-topped, parasol shaped thorn tree has the most amazing properties. The tiny green variegated leaves populate long stringy branches to give a thick, yet translucent shade. Resting under their canopy, in the dry season heat of the day, is like sitting under a waterfall of light, sound, and smells. As the breeze blows, tiny dots of intense sunlight filter through the foliage randomly, never staying long enough to scorch those protected below.

The wind through the thorns, whistling just beyond perception, soothes the parched mind, quieting the soul. When the trees blossom after the rains, the fragrance from their delicate white flowers sweetly scents the air with perfume. These trees are infused with magic. Combined with the earthy musk of animals who also frequent their shade, the trees embody the sensuality of Eden.

The crooked limbs of indigenous trees harbor birds of the most amazing blues, yellows and pied patterns. Carolyn and I took up birdwatching in the US just a few years before the sojourn to East Africa. I was astounded by the African birds' variety of color, diversity of shape, and lack of fear of humans. The Yellow Billed Hornbill, for example, with a banana shape and colored bill, contrasting black and white body and long tail, hopped about mid-strata. A constant companion, it clucked like a contented chicken as it jumped from branch to branch in the acacia tree just outside our house in the refugee camp.

The metallic bluish-green flashes of the sun off the wings of Little Purple-Banded Sunbirds were a sight to behold. With a delicate, long curved bill, this miniscule bird flits from tree to bush looking for nectar. This tiny bit of joy greeted us at the Mennonite Guest House in Nairobi when we were on leave. Amusing our desert sand-tired eyes with swatches of primary color, it was a constant presence in the cool of the evening while we sipped hot tea. We delighted in its quiet urgency, flitting from flower to flower.

In all my years in Africa, I identified over 500 bird species from the eight-foot-tall Ostrich to the tiny, tailless three-inch Crombec. The contemplative pleasure of watching the birds around me morphed into a quest to tally as many species as possible. I became a "twitcher" as the Brits call it: people who look for birds only to increase their tally, not actually spending the time communing with the avifauna. Now I've "twitched" more than 1150 species on five different continents. What is it about accumulating a raw number rather than watching for the sheer enjoyment? Perhaps it is time to stop counting and return to the joy of observing the living color, diversity and behavior of the birds around me.

Acacia trees have another use in the bushlands. If the branches are cut off, their needle-sharp thorns make an impassable barrier when placed side by side in a wide ring. Positioning the thickest woody part of the branch toward the inner circle creates a wall of outward facing jaggers. It is impenetrable without significant bodily harm for both two- and four-legged animals. The more branches placed side by side, the larger the inner protected zone becomes. A vegetable garden inside the circle will be secured from wandering, opportunistic goats who would be happy to strip clean fruit and vegetable stalks alike.

I have come to see the thorn tree wall as a metaphor for my younger heart. The constant moving as a child, the ripping up of roots put down in friendships, and perpetual adjustment to another new place isolated me. Few could get in except where I pulled the branches aside and made the opening. Now that I understand that vulnerability is the key to happiness, my task is dismantling the prickly protections of my heart.

I am grateful for the insights and memories the wildness of the Somali bush evokes even though I was under duress, uncertainty, and pain for much of the time. I now recognize that the environmental lessons that Somalia showed me nurtured a deeper spirituality. This sentiment was relayed to friends and family in one of our first form letters home.

Desertification in process

Carolyn and I are enjoying the Somali appreciation for nature. They don't seem to spend time worrying about events they have no control over i.e., weather, life, death etc. However, when there is cause for rejoicing, recognition is given to God. They have a saying *Inshallah* –if God wills– which they use on every occasion. This is a challenge for us to slow down and reconsider our own dependence on the Higher Power. — spring 1987, drafted and sent from Nairobi, Kenya

Human impact

The coastal waters of East Africa were as rich with marine life as the land was with birdlife. The iridescent blues and yellows, the camouflaged orange, browns and reds, the striped black-and-white of fish, eels, and octopi flashed before the mercurial airspace trapped in our dive masks. Snorkeling: God's underwater birdwatching.

During my tenure in Somalia, the coastal sands were not yet littered with plastic pollution that now plague every beach in the world. I remember camping on the shoreline, just outside the southern Somali town of Kismayo with a group of development workers.

As the sun set behind us, we gazed out over the reddening swells of the Indian Ocean. A German camper in our group guzzled a Heineken. After downing the beer, he crushed the aluminum with his fist and maliciously threw the can into the bushes, drunkenly blurting out, "Somebody has to be the first to fuck up this beach."

The impact of humans' avarice and futility, like my German acquaintance's littering, was rapidly making gash marks on both the sea and land. Whenever I flew over the immense Somali countryside enroute from one place to another, I saw with horror the vast concentric rings of missing trees around refugee camps. The wood cut for cooking fuel by women scouring further from their temporary places of refuge from war reminded me of locusts stripping the lands. The virgin acacia forests were being completely cleared, leaving the fragile soil to the erosive forces of sun, wind, and water.

What little health remained in the sandy ground inevitably became desert. In some areas of the countryside, soaring dunes of sand a hundred feet high drifted out across the clear-cut land.

Women carrying firewood from a distance

All was not lost. I observed firsthand that life is tenacious. Where the land looked like a moonscape around the refugee camps, amazing things sprang forth with the first drops of the twice-yearly monsoons. A smell like no other is etched in my olfactory memory. At the start of the seasonal drenching, a sweet, dusty smell is pushed before a curtain of rain. Dry, lifeless, yellow heat burning the inside of my nostrils yielded to a damp, fragrant sweetness with the approaching torrent. The temperature dropped noticeably against my cheek as the moisture cooled the surroundings, as if all creation heaved a great sigh of relief at the start of a new life cycle.

The transformation these rains brought was astounding as the bushlands throughout the Horn of Africa exploded in a riot of verdant life. Gaunt animals lost their striped bony ribcages as they fattened from the eruption of green everywhere. Nomads confined to stay close to wells with camels, cows, goats, and sheep in the dry season were liberated from thirsty tethers to roam further afield.

Deep into the bush, the rains provided democratized water, free to all in a multitude of puddles.

I remember how this transformation brought us all hope, how the refugee children rejoiced. It is the smell and feel and touch of resurrection itself. The tenacity of life is something I still cling to whenever the hungry season of political, economic, and social conditions threatens to desiccate my spirit.

A sizable number of Somali people depended on the health of animal herds. The bi-annual cycle of rains embedded themselves culturally. The Somali greeting, *bash bash iyo barwaaqo*, translated literally means "splash-splash and fortune/affluence." Figuratively it means: When the rains come, plants grow, animals get fat, have offspring, and produce lots of milk. It is a time of plenty. *Nabad iyo aano*, another greeting, literally means "peace and milk." Figuratively again, it infers security and plenty through good rains and abundant food. For many urban Somalis, at the time I was there, only one or two degrees of separation existed from their nomadic heritage. These linguistic artifacts kept them close to those roots.

For nomads, animals are their "wealth on the hoof," or "pad" in the case of camels. Their herds are a walking bank account accumulating year by year, as my bank balance might draw interest. In terms of risk, maybe a better analogy is the stock market. In times of good rains, the dividends shoot up. Yet, in lean times, animals die. The losses accrue.

The bartering value of animals would eventually be cashed in through slaughter, for celebration, negotiated as a dowry, exchanged as "blood money" or just monetized for much needed cash. Animals culled for monetization are driven toward the markets and ports in the urban areas.

On one occasion traveling to Mogadishu, I sat sipping sweet tea in a roadside tea stall. This cluster of houses was just one row deep along the tarmac and melted into the surrounding bushland just beyond the back of each. A nomad who joined our group caught my Somali friend's attention. They began to converse too fast for my rudimentary Somali language at that point. After a while everyone in the stall erupted in thunderous laughter. It was some minutes until I could discern the humor. It seems that this bushman had asked, "Does that white man acquire pickup trucks, like the one he is driving, as a form of wealth, like I breed and trade camels?" Once I understood, I answered, "No, but I have to brand my truck [the organizational logo was painted on the doors] as he had to brand his camel's necks to identify them." My quip evoked another round of raucous laughter.

Between Worlds

I appreciate now how wide the gulf was between worlds. To understand the harsh reality of the nomad, I needed to pay attention to the many organic cues that came my way through my senses. In so doing, I gained insights into both culture and raw survival skills of nomads.

The echoes of the natural world take me back to something magical, something that is as grounded as the earth itself. There was something basic about life then. Thirst, hunger, survival. These test the mettle of anyone. The nomads of Somalia were especially hardened in a way that I admired.

Upon my arrival for the first time in Somalia, I could still discern the echoes of the pristine coastal and bush lands. Climate change had not yet savagely knocked the seasonal rain cycle off its axis, creating the current scourge of unbearable droughts and recurring "millennial" type floods. Sure, there were always periods with too much or too little rain in this area of the world, but in the old days the resiliency of the land and nomadic population subsisting on it counted on the right amount of rain *somewhere*. The stoutness of the years of plenty held through the lean seasons, as animals were herded to the closest viable watering hole. Migration was possible because the bush lands were still vast unfettered tracts of lands not yet chunked up and fenced for agriculture. But that was changing fast as the old ways broke down at the end of the Cold War.

Even before Somalia's civil war began in the late 1980s, an often-uneasy peace overshadowed individual animosities because everyone had need of water and grazing areas. Land was a communal resource.

Land ownership meant walling off large tracts to exclude others from grazing it. Greed followed two decades of divide-and-rule style governance, breaking inter-clan hostility wide open. In these conditions, violent conflict grew like a cancer, metastasizing to all-out war.

I continue to mull over what it is about this time period that generates such melancholy for such a harshly yet beautifully sensual place. This era caused me angst from prolonged stress, frustration, and trauma, and it took work to rebuild my interior after such turmoil.

While I knew some of the prevailing issues this newly adopted home faced upon arrival, I was dispassionate and factual. As we moved to our placement in Northwest Somalia and those realities went from academic to visceral, I gradually became aware of something else new in my repertoire of sensory input: the pheromonic stink of my own fear from the looming threat of violence.

7

Northwest Somalia

IT WAS ONE OF those moments that was both comical and dumbfounding. At four in the morning while doing the obligatory formalities at the Mog airport in order to board the decrepit turboprop flight to Hargeisa, I saw it with my own eyes.

A man had loaded his hand luggage on the scanner before traversing the walk-through metal detector. His passage through the security arch set off a warning alarm. After emptying his pockets of coins, he tried it again with another telltale beep. He looped back through after taking off his watch, only to trigger the machine again. After stripping off his belt and his hat which had a small metal star on it, the warning sounded yet again. All the security and inspectors stood around scratching their heads as to what could be setting off the security scanner.

After a while, light seemed to dawn and he reached to his interior jacket pocket and pulled out a pistol. The security officials were full of relieved exclamation at finally figuring out what was vexing the detector. The man handed over the gun, security took the clip out of it, slapped on a baggage tag, and off went Mr. Passenger. Everyone was happy.

These kinds of events would be part of Carolyn's and my (dis) orientation to the country. Getting us to our assignment, a thousand miles away, to the northwest, took more forethought than the man with the pistol demonstrated!

Somalia is a huge country and the northwest part, where our service placement was to start, presented limited travel options. By air was the quickest. A thrice-weekly, three-hour flight by a decrepit old propeller driven Fokker Friendship F-27 was not cheap. Alternatively, driving took only two-and-a-half days thanks to the new Chinese-built road. But there were no fueling stations along the way so any vehicle traveling that distance had to carry multiple drums of diesel fuel with the ability to pump them from the drum into the vehicle tank. In the absence of a pump, a siphon hose could be used. Sucking diesel is not a pleasant task as I found out one time doing the dirty deed, ending up with an oily mouth full of the smelly stuff.

So, for the country reps having just received us in Mog as new workers, settling us into our assignment was a complicated business. For that first trip north, I ended up driving while Carolyn flew and met us there a few days after we arrived by vehicle. In addition to the distance, the northwest was nearly a different country having a different colonial history.

Geography Shaped by History

East Africa saw wave after wave of visitors wash up on her shores over the centuries. The regular trade winds blow one way round the Indian Ocean for half the year then shift direction 180 degrees for the other half. From China to the Indian subcontinent to the Arabian Peninsula to Southern Africa, sea farers plied the waterways peddling their goods in port cities while seeking wares from inland away from the coast. For centuries, the coastal cities were cosmopolitan crossroads.

Then, about 500 years ago, traders were replaced by invaders coming to subjugate. The first of the Europeans to come were the Portuguese in the sixteenth century. Later, in the seventeenth century, East Africa was overrun by Arab groups from the Arabian Peninsula. These Arabs were replaced by Ottoman Turks, who were replaced by Egyptians, then the Sultan of Zanzibar, and finally another round of Europeans after the opening of the Suez

Canal in 1869. Britain, Italy, and France established themselves in the Horn of Africa in the Somali areas during this era. And two Americans were on their way in January 1987.

From the granting of "independence" by the European Colonial powers after World War II, Somali-speaking areas of the Horn of Africa were chunked up into five distinct segments. The Somali areas of the Ogaden remain with Ethiopia. Britain administered northwest Somalia — current day Somaliland — and the North Eastern Province of Kenya. Italy oversaw what is present-day Somalia. France got a small hunk of land for its garrison of soldiers and naval base at the mouth of the southern Red Sea, which is present day Djibouti.

Recognizing the groundswell of independence sentiment sweeping the African continent, the United Nations initiated a ten-year program in 1950 to turn Somalia over to the Somalis. July 1, 1960 is Independence Day for Somalis of the south who were under Italian colonial rule. For Somalilanders of the northwest who were under British colonial administration, June twenty-six is Independence Day. Today the flag of Somalia, a five-pointed star on a blue background represents the five Somali-speaking areas where all Somali people are not yet in unity: Djibouti, the Ogaden, Northeastern Kenya, Somalia, and Somaliland.

Hargeisa

Hargeisa was the biggest city in the northwest part of Somalia at the time we arrived in 1987. Hargeisa, in present-day Somaliland, sits up on the escarpment at the northern end of the Rift Valley that cuts through much of East Africa. As continents drift apart in the great sweep of time, East Africa is being split in two, leaving a 1,367-mile gash in the landscape. On the northern rim of this weak spot sits the city of Hargeisa. It is a pleasant place to live in part because the elevation provides a coolness to the night air once the sun sets.

As the principal city of the area, it made sense for MCC to have a volunteer residence and guest house there. The MCC residence sat halfway up a dusty eucalyptus tree-lined hill in this high desert town. Set behind a tall outer stone wall, this colonial era stone house was reminiscent of the British administrative era. The house had a central courtyard surrounded by half a dozen rooms.

MCC rented this house for us to stay in when we left the refugee camp to go shopping and for rest and relaxation in the city. It was a welcome respite from the intensity of the camp, our ultimate residence. If one of us got sick, we would evacuate the camp and stay in Hargeisa, closer to the scarce medical help that existed in the area. It was as if we had an urban home and a rural home during the 18 months we were stationed in the northwest.

Our first task upon arrival in the northwest was to get set up in Hargeisa. It didn't take long before the rudimentary offerings of local food drove intense cravings for more exotic flavors of home. In a letter to my parents, I explained.

> I had the urge for something Western tonight. The urge was satisfied by a big bottle of ketchup. We have one given to us by some USAID friends. I didn't care how much sugar or salt was in it, it had to taste like something familiar. So, Carolyn made an omelet and I smothered it with ketchup. The small things help. We are really feeling our distance from home. —19 March 1987

We also experimented with raising our own food as relayed to my parents.

> Our coworker in Hargeisa got a goat for a multitude of reasons. We have been getting milk from it, it will serve as our garbage disposal, our lawn mower and a kind of pet. We were going to call it GE, General Electric, as in all those nifty appliances it eliminates or TORO as in the lawnmower. It will be nice to have fresh milk too. Now if we could only get one of those animals that gives corn flakes, we would be set for breakfast.
>
> Carolyn here. Just came in from checking the truck and the goat. Had to put more water in the windshield washer container in the truck and check its tires. The water level in the goat was OK and its tires will soon need

trimming. — Letter Twenty Five, 29 January 1988, Jon to parents

Having our own transport was crucial in Somalia. Weak and unreliable public transport was not up to the task of supporting our active work lives. We needed to control our travel for hauling supplies to our projects and obtaining timely sustenance. MCC, as the poorer cousin to other, better funded organizations, usually ended up driving cast off vehicles from the UN or other Non-Government Organizations (NGOs).

We had a slate grey, well-worn Series II 109 Land Rover pickup named Grover. Here I am giving insights into our transport challenges from hand-me-downs.

> The first item of agenda when we got back to Hargeisa was to rebuild the steering on our Grover Land Rover. We'd gotten the parts and I tore into it. It took 2 days. I was exhausted by the whole experience, not because it's hard. We had a manual and the right parts. We even had most of the tools, but it was the environment in which we had to work. My Kingdom for a good vice and the "specialized tools." We finally ended up going to our Christian Relief Aid (CRA) friends and they were most gracious to help us. I learned a humbling lesson; we don't live alone here . . . no matter how hard we try, we cannot exist on our own here . . . Now that we have the steering fixed on Grover all we have to fix yet are the brakes and the clutch. — April 1987

The first time we tried to fill Grover up with petrol we realized that there was no key to unlock the filler cap. Our friends from CRA, Hans and Jackie, saved the day once again by using a bolt cutter to snip off the fuel cap lock. It was not the last time these good folks bailed us out.

> We may be running out of fuel soon and we have to go to CRA, UN High Commissioner for Refugees (UNHCR) to borrow some till we get to Djibouti where I will order it from there. — 6 June 1987, letter to parents

Our fuel was purchased and stored in bulk at the UNHCR compound up the hill from our house in Hargeisa. When the city was attacked in May 1988, those fuel stores were some of the first hit by artillery from the Somali southern forces, bursting into intense flames and smoke.

To increase Grover's dismal fuel economy, we kept it in two-wheel drive. I once got this decrepit petrol-powered beast stuck in downtown Hargeisa on a sandy street where I was looking for some obscure part. Until I shifted into four-wheel drive, we just spun the tires. Getting stuck meant hopping out the squarish door, bending down at each front wheel and engaging the wheel hub locks, hopping back in the tin can cab and grinding the gears into four-wheel drive, low gear. It was a hot and arduous process just to extricate ourselves from the sandy pit misnamed a "city street." Such were the rudimentary challenges of shopping in the city.

Boiling Point

As Somali- speaking areas emerged out from under colonial control, Somaliland gained independence from its British overlords. Somaliland enjoyed the status of being its own nation for four days in July 1960 before joining the southern part of the country to unify into the greater Somalia. The northwestern clans soon regretted this arrangement, as the south sought to dominate and control all things political and economic.

The northwest was full of tension and unrest. The boiling point was fast approaching where local clans fomented a rebellion against their southern overlords. Refugees were pawns, as they were used to dilute the numerical advantage of local clans, in part through the assistance from UNHCR. The south controlled the large food shipments to the refugees, influencing local economics in favor of the Mogadishu government in the south. The refugee ration allotments were weaponized. Those in the northwest felt as if their lands were occupied by the south.

We knew only some of the serious issues this newly adopted home faced. The subtlety of clan politics, the nuance of an oral culture, and the language barriers all conspired to keep information from us. It is one thing to know these things in my head: it's another to have the hairs on the back of my neck rise when I was immersed in conflict realities. Carolyn and I had new, heightened proprioception, quickly developed when the information moved from cerebral to the hyper awareness of personal danger.

On the occasion that I had to travel to Djibouti for business, I carefully outlined our growing uneasiness with the escalating tensions. Describing the conflict in a letter through the Somali postal system seemed too risky. If this kind of mail was intercepted by the Somali authorities, they could construe our letter as speaking ill of the government, and in the worst case, accuse us of undercover activities. At this point in the tensions in the country, officials expelled expatriates for lesser accusations.

> Expats are so in the dark here. We have to listen to the BBC to hear the news. We still feel basically safe but the constant tension of the military presence and always being watched and with Somalis so paranoid I get weary and frustrated. — 20 July 1987, sent from Djibouti to Jon's parents

We moved to the northwest, already a cauldron of social disruption from hosting half a million refugees. On top of that was the building political pressure cooker from decades of divide and rule. It was in this context that we began our work in the refugee camp.

8

Refugees

AFTER FIVE MONTHS OF living out of a suitcase, language learning in Kenya, orienting to the country and outfitting for our assignment location, we finally moved "permanently" to Saba'ad Refugee Camp on June seven, 1987. Situated about twenty-five miles from Hargeisa on the Berbera road, it was very rural compared to Mogadishu and Hargeisa.

A vast infrastructure of support had been developed by the United Nations to tend to the huge number of refugees hosted in very rural parts of the country. Having been established nearly a decade before, these camps had relatively secure water supplies and a well-developed food supply chain. Even health facilities and schools had been set up. There were no fences to keep people from coming and going as they pleased. Due to better infrastructural services than the surrounding villages, many local people took up residence in the camps to obtain these benefits.

Saba'ad was one of a half-dozen camps in the northwest of Somalia that housed refugees from the Ogaden War between Somalia and Ethiopia when, in 1977, President Barre launched an attack on Ethiopia to capture the Ogaden region and force its incorporation into the Somali Republic. Somalia had the upper hand for a while until the Soviets had a change in policy and switched to equip the Ethiopians with a billion dollars in sophisticated weapons. With the aid of thousands of Cuban proxy troops, Ethiopia quickly regained all the captured Ogaden territory from the Somalis. In the process, the Ethiopian army wreaked havoc in the area, displacing many of the Ogadeni inhabitants. Between 1978 and 1985, hundreds of thousands of refugees fled across the border of Ethiopia into Somalia. At the height of the refugee crisis in 1981, the Somali Republic claimed it had up to 1.5 million refugees within its borders. These figures had been, in the past, inflated to engender more aid. The number of refugees regularly used by the UNHCR to distribute aid was 700,000. The nature of the conflict and population meant that many refugees opted to relocate to urban areas to live with relatives or friends rather than stay in the camps.

Saba'ad Refugee Camp 1987

Saba'ad Refugee Camp Compound

There were two mud brick structures in our compound on the extreme edge of the camp. From the front side of our little walled-in space was a single room house. To the left, our twelve by fourteen-foot room replete with bed, lockable storage area, and small desk. On the right side of the compound, equally large and with a slanting roof, our office. There was a central table in there for meetings and classes as well as a small cupboard for office supplies.

An open patio between the two structures had a concrete floor. A small waist-high mud wall to the back side of the compound kept curious children at bay. On the front side of these two structures was a green "shadow" as we called it, a tangle of dusty, coarse vines that made shade below. In the heat of the day, when the inside rooms reached oven temperatures from the sun pounding on their tin roofs, we were driven outside to sit on the concrete seat under the shadow.

Our outdoor kitchen area, on the right side of the shadow, was just outside the office window. The cooking area consisted of a large storage cupboard, a semi-protected area for the kerosene stove, a stand for the water filter, and the wooden countertop which had a sink installed in it. This area accumulated a thick layer of dust, dirt, and sand so rapidly that it always had to be cleaned before use. With no running water, the sink was practically useless especially when the dust and dirt blew in and fell from the shadow overhead. We only used it for holding dirty dishes and channeling wash water to a bucket below. We emptied all wash water on our garden or trees as water was scarce.

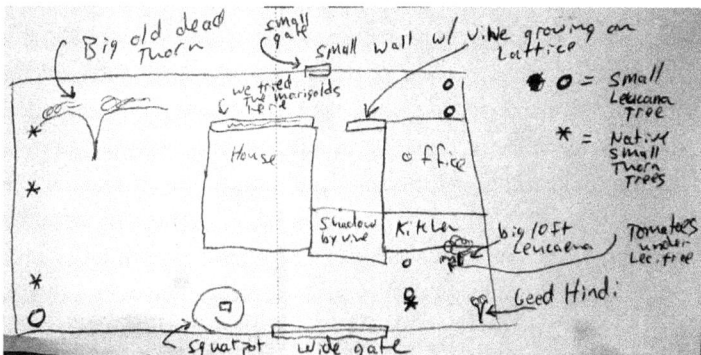

Letter Nineteen, 11 September 1987: I sent the above sketch in a letter to my parents showing where the plants were around the house in Saba'ad

When the blowing sand and ever-present dust threatened to drift completely over my spirits, I found solace in tending seedlings, hoping to nurture them into mature trees.

> Planting trees has become my savior. I have started a small nursery and hope to have some trees ready to go by spring rainy season. So, the green things are soothing my mind and as I pour water of life on the trees my love goes in too. — 29 September 1987, Jon's letter to parents

Sanitation

The first thing I noticed about our new home in the camp was the outhouse, or *musqusha* [mus Q sha] in Somali. The loo, as the Brits call it, was shaped like a conch shell. Holding off as long as possible, I finally yielded to the call of nature. Entering from just inside our mud brick wall, I walked the few steps around the spiral until I was in the inner part of the large maze-like circle of mud brick walls. An ingenious design that eliminated the need for a door, the blowing wind created some irritating ventilation. A big gust of wind, funneled in by the twirl of the entry wall, would whip the accumulated sand and dirt into our face as we did our business.

Smack in the center was a large book-sized beveled block with a wire loop nailed on top. Pulling this up unsealed the slightly smaller gash in the concrete pad where the unmentionables went. A blizzard of black-green poop flies as we called them, exploded from their dank, dark dungeon to alight everywhere outside. An army of cockroaches scuttled away from the hole back into the darkness of the pit. The familiar tickle of tiny wings and antenna on my backside was unavoidable. There were no hand railings for the squat pot for my weak yet to be conditioned knees. There was no toilet paper dispenser. There was no reading material to occupy our time, only drifts of sand below and open sky above. Looking up was a much better option to stare at than down at the wildlife teeming below. Carolyn described her experience in using the "facilities."

The biggest bug challenge faced yet is when I have to pee in the middle of the night. I take the flashlight and gingerly step into the open-air outhouse only to find the corners crawling with <u>large</u> cockroaches. There is simply no use getting [the] willies over them cuz they're there and I gotta go and they won't go away. So, I just stomp on the cement around the hole, quickly squat hoping those long antennas don't wave in the air and tickle my fanny. It's really too bad. Cuz instead of hurrying, I *could* be enjoying the gorgeous stars overhead. I usually use my skirt as a nose cover. — Carolyn's letter to her parents, 23 April 1987

Cleaning of hands after the squat pot was a luxury I decided we would just have to have. We had a bucket with a spigot near our small postage-stamp garden. Doing double duty—it was hung over our garden watering the plants while washing hands—it required filling every few days.

MCC Compound we called home at Saba'ad Camp 1987 — note the spiral squat pot

My assumptions about cleanliness were quickly checked as I was admonished early on to the *faux paus* of ambidexterity. "In Somalia, you reserve the left hand for unwashed things," instructed Sala'ad the MCC Mog office helper. "Never shake hands, eat, hand food to another, or pat another shoulder with the left hand," he instructed. That is in case there is no wash water. Heaven help the "south paw" in such a culture.

Because of Oxfam, a UK-based organization that specialized in water resources, the camp had access to clean water. At first, we carried water in plastic five-gallon jugs from the water source a half-mile away just as refugees did. That really drove home how much energy and time it took to do the most basic culinary and hygienic activities. I gained a little insight into the emotional toll it must take to have to hike miles for water that was dirty and might contain parasites and disease.

Later in our stay, we hired a donkey cart to deliver a fifty-five-gallon drum of water every other day. Half we poured on our little postage stamp garden to extend the growing of our spindly vegetables a few more days. The other half was our drinking, cooking, washing, and bathing water for two days. That meant that we used roughly five gallons of water per person per day. An extravagant luxury by the standards of the camp since refugees, walking half a mile to the well, could only carry home a few gallons for a whole household per day.

Water delivery to the MCC compound by donkey cart,
Saba'ad Refugee Camp 1987

When Carolyn and I discovered a wiggling, tiny worm-like mosquito larva in the drinking water barrel one day, we were at first consternated. How could mosquitoes breed in water that was so regularly cycled through with cooking and drinking? How could they reproduce so fast? Lastly, should they be strained out or would it just be better to add a bit of protein to our thirst quenching? From locals, we learned that they were harmless, so we just learned to drink and not look too closely.

Illness

At first, our health seemed to track the harshness of the seasons, which in turn influenced our diet. Diarrhea came with the rains, as the runoff swept the bacteria and parasites into the wells where drinking water came from. But actually, diarrhea also came with the dry season as the wells receded and bacteria and parasites were more concentrated in what little water was to be found. We realized that what made us ill was random and could strike either slowly or quickly.

I once got giardia from who knows where. Unmistakable in symptoms, I will spare you the details except to say the color and consistency of giardia-laden diarrhea can't be misdiagnosed. In addition, I once had vertigo so bad I could not stand. That passed in a few days.

So many of the bugs we could get were almost as bad as their prophylactics or cures. The latest and greatest anti-malarial of that era, Mefloquine, caused wild hallucinogenic nightmares.

Carolyn had her share of gut bugs too. She got whammied by typhoid in August 1988, taking three months to recover her strength, recuperating in the Mennonite Guest House in Nairobi.

Food

The food options here aren't very good. The market has only a few tomatoes and an occasional papaya. Our staples are rice and pasta. The sauce is usually pretty slim. We do get the fresh veggies in Hargeisa, but we are only going in once a week, because when we go in it usually takes at least two to three days to "take care of business."

My main starch was bread, little French type pieces, but
now that the Saba'ad Baker has gone, so no more bread.
The bakery may be reopened with the help of an MCC
small business loan. Eggs are getting scarce here because
it is the season where they don't lay very many. We pay
about $0.10 for each of them. We don't eat meat because
it's not easily available to us. I think it would do some
good to find some though. — 31 July 1987, Jon's letter
to parents

Life and work in the refugee camp was both physically and
emotionally taxing. I was weakened from the heat, dust, and low
caloric intake. The food we got was bland staples such as rice and
pasta. Very few condiments to add to those staples were available.
The one tiny shop in camp had a few small cans of tomato paste
and a few tins of sardines on its lone shelf. That was the extent of
it, save a few sweet biscuits from an Arab Emirate. Raw fruits and
vegetables were seasonal, but only slightly more abundant.

Economics 101—The Watermelon

On one hot dusty day in the place we called home, as did 40,000
others the world labeled refugees, we took a walk. Being relatively
new to the camp, Carolyn and I decided to go check out the market
to see what we could buy locally and what we would have to
fetch twenty-five miles down the road in Hargeisa. Two out-of-
place white North Americans walking through the camp attracted
a lot of attention. To children's taunts of *gal gal*, assuming we were
infidels, and the stares from adults, we strolled the half-mile to
the "market." This was a bit of a misnomer because there was precious little extra wealth in circulation at the camp to buy anything.
The true currency for refugees was the food rations of corn and
oil. What was not used for sustenance found its way to the major
towns around and was sold or bartered for other necessities. The
"market" in our camp contained a few women selling some vegetables that were grown in gardens near the camp.

On this day as we passed by, there was a third of a watermelon in front of a woman seller waiting patiently, with others, to sell her meager allotments. Carolyn and I, dried out from the hot blasts of wind off the rocky plain, were delighted to see the beautiful red and white of the flayed-open melon.

We promptly asked, in our halting Somali, how much per slice? We greedily calculated what the whole chunk would cost and whipped out our cash, paid for the melon, and walked off to the bewilderment of the market vendors. We did not understand the uproar that purchase left behind, until much later. The only melon for miles, this was a delicacy, carefully sliced up and offered to anyone with just a few shillings. Our disposable wealth precluded anyone else from sharing the joys of its cooling refreshment and deprived the seller of the joy and pride of slowly doling out a treat among the community.

Calorie Count

On a break from hot, dusty refugee camp life, we traveled to the riot of green in the cool highlands of Nairobi, Kenya for rest and relaxation. For Carolyn this break was very welcome. She was relieved to don a sleeveless dress and shed her head scarf, an effort to be culturally sensitive to Islamic traditions while in Somalia. In a haunting picture from that time, she stands beside me happy to be free from ugly and hot attire. I, on the other hand, look gaunt, almost as if I had come from a concentration camp. A big beard overwhelms what is visible of my face. Feeling my life force ebbing away, I did a calorie count and realized I was only consuming 1400 calories a day.

Carolyn and Jon Rudy at the Nairobi Mennonite Guest House in 1988

Upon returning to Somalia from respite in Kenya, our director suggested we go to the refugee camp meat market for a hunk of animal flesh every once in a while. Without refrigeration, though, I wondered how we would keep from getting food poisoning.

The meat market on the fringes of the camp was not hard to find due to the smell of rotting meat, the flies, and the bustle of buyers and sellers. Chunks of the daily slaughter — goat, cow, sheep, camel — hung from hooks in the sun. Once I saw the unsanitary conditions, I was even more worried about spoiled food making us sick.

We solved that problem by buying early in the morning and then placing the meat in a vinegar, salt, and oil marinade. From the morning when we purchased it in the camp market, it sat sealed in a dark cupboard, the coolest place in our compound, till dusk when we cooked the meat. The marinade helped to soften up those toughened aged beasts slaughtered that week. I suspected that it was an artform the nomads had perfected: driving the oldest camel to slaughter and arriving ten minutes before it dropped dead of old age. Such was the quality of what could be purchased in the camp under the guise of meat.

Buying Camel's Milk From the Woman on the Rural Road

We were speeding through the bush on one of Somalia's main roads that I liked to call the chute. For endless mile upon mile the black paint on sand, as some called the hastily made tarmac track, ran straight. On either side nearly up to the blacktop was a thicket of trees, brush, and foliage. It was like careening through a green tunnel except for the bright blue sky above.

We triad of MCCers were many miles from the nearest town, having left the camp early, sans breakfast, to beat the inevitable heat. Having been a few hours on this eternal stretch of bush, hunger set in. Suddenly we came upon and then passed a woman walking along the road bearing a wooden container filled with camel's milk. She was headed in the direction of the nearest town, maybe ten miles away. One of us in the car suggested that we turn around and buy that whole container for breakfast, reminding us that the milk of the one-humped dromedary was a nutritionally complete meal. After all, Somali youth proved their manhood by taking the camels deep into the bush for months and surviving off the milk alone.

So, we stopped and offered to buy the milk, compensating her generously. The woman hesitatingly accepted. The three of us up-ended the smoke-darkened wooden milk jug and polished off what must have been nearly two gallons of milk. The effect of the warm, smoky milk did indeed satiate us for the rest of the morning.

As we sped off to our destination, I turned and looked at our breakfast provider. She had a lost look about her. She was in a quandary about the day's task ahead of her. She had planned to walk the long distance to the nearest town market, peddle her milk, and perhaps buy supplies for the clan back in the bush who were caring for the rest of the animals. Now, having been "relieved" of a major task, she was at a loss for what to do next. Our needs had upset her routine, and she was genuinely perplexed about how to proceed.

In my mind it was a simple transaction of money for goods, but I wondered years later if had we done her violence in some way. Had my attitude toward commerce and my accompanying wealth been the point of the globalization spear that pierced her world for the worse?

Letters, Letters, Letters

It is hard to imagine now with cell phones and internet just how inefficient and time-delayed our communication was to loved ones back home. When we started our service in Somalia in 1987, the MCC office in Mogadishu had no telephone, no fax machine, and no two-way radio. A thrice-weekly telex from the reps to the home office was sent from a hotel half an hour's walk downtown from the MCC office. In an emergency, the reps could drive to the UN offices and send a radio gram via shortwave radio to the nearest UN field office, who held it for us to pick up. Slower printed mail and incoming post was sent by air in the UN secure pouch. Thus, a round trip letter and response to/from home sometimes took a month. Ask a question . . . wait . . . wait . . . wait . . . get an answer.

> I must say after the dry spell of not getting letters from you for a month, I was very excited to get two. I don't think I sufficiently appreciated the regular letters and our weekly phone calls while in the US. Now I am so thankful for your vigilant writing. It means very much. — 31 July 1987, Jon's letter to parents

We had an enormous amount of down time when we were not engaged in our primary jobs in the camp. We empathized with refugees who, due to fleeing war, had put their lives on hold in a place where, beyond survival, there was not much to do.

We filled our time with writing missives to parents and siblings. Our sole means of communication was by letters. Aerograms were the cheapest way to send a letter. They were tissue paper thin and, when written on both sides, the ink bled through to the other side making them difficult to read. We waited for the next word from home to measure all the losses that kept stacking up. Putting Midgy, the beloved family dog down, missed weddings, missed funerals, the coming of spring, and so many other things that mud bricks, flies, and the stares of disheveled children could never make up.

We had to be careful sending letters, though. We never knew who was reading them as they exited the country, or if they ever got to where they were going. Carolyn's mother started numbering the letters she sent so that we could track if any went missing. Because this was the Cold War, the global clash of empires was felt, in part, through the insecurity of our mail.

As if to drive this point home, long after we left Somalia, having moved back to the US, a strange letter arrived via the post. It contained a dirty, crumpled, torn-open envelope that a friend tried to send to us years earlier. It had been mailed to us by a US soldier who was in Mogadishu during the US humanitarian mission in 1993 (think *Blackhawk Down* era). Inside was an explanation. It read:

> UNLSC-S Comptroller, Unit 00
> APO AE 09898-0800
> 22 May 1993
>
> Concerned Citizen,
>
> I am an [US] army officer currently stationed in Somalia. I recently walked through the ruins of the people's Palace in Mogadishu. One of the rooms I walked into was a mailroom. Located on the floor was your envelope to a letter (I could not find the letter), along with tens of thousands of other letters, that was [sic] sent in 1987. I thought you might like to have it returned.
>
> I hope the address on the envelopes will still reach you but that is questionable since it is 6 years old.

sincerely CPT Lee E Hanson

Having never gotten this letter, we confirmed our suspicions that the Somali security apparatus was scanning our incoming and outgoing mail.

9

Camp Routine

OUR LIVES IN THE camp never seemed to have a predictable routine. Our expectations of what life would be like were shaped by two things: first, our US life as we worked, studied or relaxed, and secondly, the job description provided by MCC to recruit us. MCC advertised running a skills training program for me and community health for Carolyn, but our day-to-day life had little semblance to that job description.

Waiting, Observation, Disconnect and Empathy

What was not advertised as part of the job was the waiting. Waiting for the supplies for the training project. Waiting for the participants to arrive. Waiting for the health team to include Carolyn in their activities.

Waiting was a mental discipline we had a lot of opportunity to practice. Yet our waiting paled in comparison to the refugees who had their lives on hold for ten years, waiting to go somewhere, to go home, to be repatriated to another country, to start meaningful work, waiting on permissions, waiting for rations, or the wait for rains. The waiting gave us both the opportunity to practice new powers of observation and introspection.

It seems as if we're waiting here. We are waiting with these displaced people for something. We get promises from the agencies helping "poor refugees," but they are like the treaties between the US government and the native population of the North American continent, broken at the government's whim. So, we wait. It seems the camp wakes in the same way it has for the past eight years. It goes to bed in the same way it has always gone to bed. The sheep and the goats come and go every day and the babies are born. I believe it is good for me to have this routine, although I'm usually not so contemplative about it. Sometimes . . . most times it drives me crazy. — 12 August 1987, Jon's letter to parents

As time slowed down and the days stretched, we developed a new connection to the natural world round us.

We have been in the camp it seems like a year or so but I think it's only been 2 weeks. That it is mid-August has no meaning here. We do notice the moon and its phases, and the seasons seem to be changing. It is getting a bit cooler in the daytime and at night we are down to just having one window open instead of two. — 12 August 1987, Jon's letter to parents

And the increasing disconnect from our families brought a new empathy for those around us and appreciation for ways of keeping in touch.

It has been over six weeks and we still have not heard a peep about Rosie's [Carolyn's sister] wedding. So, this too is part of our waiting and empathizing with the refugees. We do not know of our families any more than some of them. One man here told me the other day has not heard of his family in ten years. He knows not whether they are dead or alive. We at least assume our families are alive, we have the power of fast communications at our disposal if we needed it. They have the oral tradition carried by the nomads. Sometimes I think that way is more effective and reliable. — 12 August 1987, Jon's letter to parents

Living on Display

While waiting to do something, we realized that we needed to strengthen the relationships with the people around us. There were always people around us. With little for the refugees to do, anything new — us — attracted attention. Carolyn's perspective on the people differed from mine. Carolyn wrote:

> The biggest adjustment here will not be the dirt. Instead, it will be the "open living" that is expected of us. People come and sit under our shadow [shaded area for sitting outside] and kids hang over the wall staring until our guard throws stones at them [to chase them away]. A few will leave when I kindly say goodbye to them. We're not sure if this continual stream will continue or if it is more or less the welcoming parties. It does make us feel welcome, though, and I guess we can be glad they don't arrive before 7:30 AM and they usually stay away from 1:00 to 3:00 PM and after it's dark. — Carolyn's letter to her parents, 10 June 1987, from Saba'ad Refugee Camp

While I wrote:

> We have people coming through our compound all the time. Sometimes people come by in tens and all just sit and talk, or practice English. I am exhausted by all the people who come. Carolyn is better at coping with living such a "public life" than I. Sometimes I just get grouchy and want them all to go away and mind their own business. People are constantly calling us the names of the previous couple that was here under MCC. So, we deal with identity issues as well. We are in the process of building a brick fence around our little house which will keep the donkeys and the goats out of our yard because they eat our trees. I'm also hoping that it gives us a little privacy. There are very few expatriate organizations that live in the refugee camp and we are the only non- Somali/refugee people in the camp, so we are a novelty. — 20 June 1987 letter to Jon's parents

Hi, I'm Frank

While we waited, we had ample opportunity to visit with residents of the camp. As a deep introvert, the constant stream of people through our compound was taxing, especially with the constant barrage of questions and, what seemed to me, very unfiltered comments.

"Why don't you have children yet?" queried our friend Abdi. "Maybe Jon isn't preparing himself well enough." What these "preparations" were, we were too shy to ask so could only speculate, assuming it had to do with eating or drinking some kind of aphrodisiac. But couples our age without children were viewed with pity: something was wrong. By now we should have a whole gaggle of our own children streaming behind us as we walked through the camp.

We had gotten used to blunt questions. There is a saying; "it doesn't hurt to ask." Once we had a refugee ask us an amazingly simple question, "Can I have your truck?" It doesn't hurt to ask, it costs nothing. If the answer is "yes" then so much the better. Nothing lost with a "no." Blunt and outlandish questions kept coming. Like this conversation, many of our interactions were layered with complexity or nuance, a Somali linguistic tradition.

Honor Guard – Hussein

In the refugee camp, we needed to hire a guard in part because it was, well, culturally expected. We had a truck, access to resources and programmatic oversight, so the common cultural understanding was that we needed to provide a job to someone to look after those things when our gaze was elsewhere. We heard it said that in this part of the world, one third of the people guard one third of the people against one third of the people. That is a pretty cynical view of at least one of those parts of the triad.

Hussein was our guard in Saba'ad Refugee Camp. We inherited his services from the previous volunteers. Hussein, a man in his 40's, had fled his home in Ethiopia's Ogaden region when the

Ethiopian soldiers routed the Somali army a decade before. Hired by previous MCCers, he was loyal to his job for MCC as we were to find out.

Hussein the MCC guard at Saba'ad Refugee Camp in 1987

Hussein's tiny guard house was barely big enough for a bed. It sat 150 feet away from our house out on its own with not a single shade tree around. Hussein would sit in there on hot summer days, roasting under the tin roof. He wore a wraparound cloth, called a *macawiis*. To this day, I can see him sitting there in my mind's eye, cracking sunflower seeds between his teeth, just biding his time. He had a spear as the sole means of identification as a guard.

One hot, windless afternoon, Carolyn and I were sitting out-side under our shadow lazily visiting with friends. Hussein was praying in his guard house a stone's throw away. Suddenly, we saw the dust devils of four or five vehicles plowing through the main street of camp. They skidded to a stop up in front of our gate and soldiers with AK-47s jumped out. In the middle car was the American ambassador and his wife. They had heard that there were some Americans living in the refugee camp and had come for a quick visit to say hi and to see where we lived. We could barely convince the diplomats to sit down and have a cup of water before they jumped back in their car and sped off.

After the dust cleared and everyone left, we noticed that Hussein, in the middle of the initial confusion, had run over with his spear to protect us. One spear against a dozen machine guns. To this day we wonder what Hussein would have done if the rifles would have been pointed at us with intent to harm. Our main takeaway was insight into Hussein's sense of loyalty in taking his job seriously and to the extreme.

Among the Elements

The windswept plains of rural Somalia where refugee camps were situated became wastelands. Where once was thick foliage of thorn trees, only skeletons of stripped branches, tree stumps, and spindly ground covers remained. People cut trees for cooking fuel, denuding the richness of this land.

No one was to blame unless it was the arms dealers. Peddling their wares of death to anyone who wanted power at the barrel of a gun, they uncaringly pushed death to whoever would buy. Making refugees was a consequence they ignored in their quest for profits and power.

The results of easily accessible weapons, even today, are large clumps of displaced people who huddle under whatever is available for shelter. Feed sacks cobbled together, a tarp here and there from the UN Refugee agency. They scramble for survival, making use of anything at hand. In the case of much of sub-Saharan Africa, cutting trees is still the only way to cook food.

For cooking, a pot was tenuously balanced atop three rocks. With white maize or rice bubbling inside, the limbs hacked from the nearest tree were gradually pushed in from all sides as the fire consumed the wood, heating the pot. The circles of denuded land spread ever outward with time, as women gathered the cooking fuel for sustenance. The diversity of the Somali bush consumed, one belly-full at a time.

With the trees gone, winds swept down over the pile of rocks outside the camp before the rains came. Monsoon winds shifted their ancient pattern in this scoured land. Blowing one way half the year, they reversed course the other half. When they did shift, rains followed.

Windswept camp conditions

With the trees gone, the winds blew unimpeded across the land, whipping up fine sand that invaded everything. What once was a still, serene panorama became a wild, stinging wind full of grit. Sand became a spice that seasoned all food on the plate. It does no good to raise a fist, shaking to the gods of the sky, "I am not a chicken, I have no gizzard to grind your powdered rocks and stones!" Resigned, I huddled over food, protecting my eyes and plate from the next onslaught of dirt-laden wind. And when the wind stopped, the ever-present hordes of flies descended.

> Nature has been very trying on us lately. The wind has been blowing almost constantly at 10 to 25 mph and that gets tiring especially when we can't get away from the noise and dust it picks up. I have been feeling very

tired and rundown, lethargic in the last few days. I have
a combination of two things I think causes it. Part is the
above conditions we live with. The flies here require us so
much energy to shoo them away, especially the kind that
crawl unabashed into your nose and mouth and eyes.
—31 July 1987, Jon's letter to parents

As we grew acclimated to these harsh conditions, we noticed
some beauty between wind blasts and fly plagues. We came to appreciate our natural surroundings and find hope and beauty in the
small things.

Some things that give us hope: our faithful staff, our two
lone trees that fight for survival, the occasional new birds
that take a few minutes to rest on our dead thorn tree, the
tiny marigolds pushing through the hard soil in hopes
of bringing some color to our brown surroundings. The
darling neighbor kids who call us by name instead of
"white person," the gorgeous, cool evening sky after a
hot bothersome day. — Letter to family and friends, 7
August 1987

Wildlife

Just outside the vast cluster of hovels that made up the refugee
camp, wild animals still roamed the haunted rocks and crevices,
sometimes making their presence known. The "whoup whoup" of
the *warabi*—hyena—as they thundered clumsily by our mud brick
wall in the darkness reminded us how close we were to those un-
tamed natives.

One morning, before the camp fully awoke, we took a walk
to the distant rock out cropping and saw a strange little mouse-
sized creature with a furry bob on its tail. Hopping like a miniature
kangaroo, it scurried before us to disappear into the dawn light.
For thirty-two years we assumed what we saw on those haunted
rocks in northwest Somalia were the ghosts and echoes of previous
magic that was nearly palpable on those forlorn plains, its aberra-
tion only visible at half-light out of the corner of our eye. Science

has a more pedestrian yet intriguing answer. It was only in August 2020 that I stumbled onto reporting of research that confirmed the presence of this tiny mammal, the *Somali sengi*. I saw an article in the *Guardian* which led me to correspond with the researcher.

From: Jon
Sent: Friday, August 21, 2020, 8:05 AM
To: Steven Heritage
Subject: Somali sengi

Steven greetings. I saw the press on the rediscovery of the Somali sengi. Congrats on documenting this animal.

My wife and I were aid workers in the Saba'ad Refugee Camp outside Hargeisa on the road to Berbera from 1987 to May 1988 up to the start of the civil war. We had a house on the outskirts of camp and went walking one dawn at sunrise. We saw this little animal but were unable to find any information about it then. We had only a tourist guide of mammals in East Africa but other queries gave us nothing to go on. Your article confirmed this is what we saw. The defining feature in the dawn light was the tuft on its long tail. It was unmistakable.

Anyway, thought this sighting might help you fill in the info. Would be happy to provide more details if you like.

Jonathan Rudy
Manheim, Pennsylvania

Subject: Re: Somali sengi
Date: Sat, 22 Aug 2020 11:16:10 +0000
From: Steven Heritage
To: Jon

Hi Jonathan,

Thanks for your nice message which made me smile!

Almost certainly, the species that you saw in 1987/1988 is the one getting all the attention now. While we only have recent scientific data from Djibouti, I have confidence that the species is also currently widespread and thriving in Somalia – particularly after hearing reports like this from you and others. We are sure that the missing data about this little mammal (and several other plants and animals in the HoA) is attributable to a lack of reporting and scientific research, and not due to the species being rare.

The Djiboutian ecologists that we collaborated with are recording their wildlife information and reporting it to their government as a measure of the health of biodiversity in the country. They are also extending invitations to international scientists. I wish these situations were more broadly embraced throughout the region. But, of course, I realize that there might be other priorities.

Thanks again for sharing your story. I find it fascinating to hear about an animal sighting from so many years ago. Please feel free to get in touch any time.

Cheers my friend!
Steven
Steven Heritage
Duke University
Duke Lemur Center, Division of Fossil Primates
1013 Broad Street, Durham, NC 27705

Bruce and the Crocodile

"Wildlife" could also refer to, in retrospect, that we lived a very wild life partly from all the bizarre things that happened unexpectedly. The extremes of monotony of everyday life were punctuated by some very wild personalities and situations that went with the terrain.

Bruce, a big, strapping, red-haired Canadian, was also an MCC volunteer at the time we were there. He and Cathy his wife had been in the southern refugee camps a year already by the time we visited them for the first time. I always wished that I had Bruce's boundless energy and positive can-do attitude. A farmer, he tried to take his understanding of crop management into the Somali Bush. He got busy with irrigation projects since the soil was so porous and sandy. He took quite quickly to tropical plants such as bananas, mango trees, and other fruit-bearing plants. He was always ready to try something new and not afraid to innovate when something was not working, fixing his failures.

The compound he and Cathy had created in one short year was nothing short of a miracle, an Eden along the Juba River contrasting to the wind-blown treeless surroundings. It had cool tree cover and produced fruits and vegetables they consumed in their meals.

On one sultry occasion we were walking out in the fields among the irrigation ditches. The flowing water pumped from the river created green gardens. Bruce was in bare feet wading through the irrigation ditch water to cool his feet. All at once he exclaimed, "I think there's something in here!" Walking a little further he exclaimed even louder, "I know there's something in here!"

Reaching down, he pulled out an eighteen-inch-long baby crocodile. It had been nibbling on his toes as he waded.

Islam Saving People in Makomani Village

Later in our assignment, after evacuating the north, we worked in the south. I had been working with water and sanitation issues in the Lower Juba Region of Somalia only a few months when a unique request came to me.

My counterpart, Abdirashid, and I were visiting a quaint village called Makomani on the Juba River about fifteen miles from the regional capital of Kismayo. It consisted of thirty or so stick-and-thatch homes and a shop that had the basic things for sale like rice, pasta, tomato sauce, matches, cigarettes, soap, etc. We had gone to investigate the possibilities of doing a latrine promotion project in this village. While there, the villagers asked us if we would put a well in their town.

We noted that the women of the village walked one-hundred yards upstream to the river to fetch water. We also noted that they used the downstream part of the river as bathing, washing and bathroom facilities. Now that's okay, except that the village downstream does the same thing, draws water from upstream and uses downstream for hygiene. The people of Makomani did not complain about dirty water; in fact, they liked the taste of the muddy water better than that which came from a neighboring well. It was just that crocodiles would take two village women a year when they drew water on the riverbanks.

The United Nations Children's Fund (UNICEF) who I was seconded to at this point, had no money for this project. MCC, who I worked for, had no money for this project. The people of Makomani had no money for this project, but they had the will. When I visited the town a few months later, the village men had completed a hand-dug sweet water well near the mosque for the purpose of mandatory ablutions before prayers. As a side benefit, the women of the village also were able to draw water for domestic use.

It can be said that Islam was saving at least two women a year in Makomani.

Darkness Falls on the Camp

As we adjusted to the new cadence of camp life, we slowed down to the ageless, patient pace of the sun and moon.

> I'm turning into a chicken; I want to sleep the minute the sun sets. The only difference is I don't exactly feel like crowing at 6:00 AM. — Carolyn's letter to parents, 10 June 1987 from Saba'ad Camp

There was a time in the evening when the sun slipped behind the rocks in the distance. As the sky darkened, the sandy soil brightened with the remaining light and illuminated the surroundings with an orange glow. A hush descended on the refugee camp like a collective sigh, as if to say, one more difficult day done in the struggle of life.

By the onset of deep darkness, the silence covered us like a blanket. The human-made noises gave way to sounds from the natural world. Our symphonic lullaby was the chirping of crickets, the wind through our dead thorn tree, or the yelping of the hyenas in the distance.

In the dense darkness that followed there was little to do after dinner had been consumed. With no streetlights, what little light we could see came from cooking fires, candles, or flashlights that were held privately in the confines of each dwelling. Wood, kerosene, and batteries were expensive commodities, making light a valuable resource not to be wasted by spilling it out where it was of no use. Of course, the moon shone most nights during its waxing. The skies usually cleared of clouds by dusk.

Being close to the equator, half of our twenty-four-hour day was in relative darkness. Carolyn and I would go out on our small patio, eat supper and turn on the news. The shortwave radio brought us the BBC World Service which beamed to all East Africa. Each evening we perked up our ears for any news of Somalia.

One of the frustrating things about Somalia at that time was finding reliable and timely news. We found BBC to be one of the most accurate and honest places to get information about what was happening in the very country where we were sitting.

Another evening ritual was to have a flossing party. Tough stringy, camel's meat packed the spaces between our teeth necessitating a cleaning every evening. As we sat in the dark with our backs against the warm mud brick wall of our one room dwelling, still radiating heat from the afternoon sun, we would pass the dental floss around.

Gazing up at the stars, we would see tiny pinpricks of light scattered across the sky. Set against the frozen antiquity of the Milky Way, constellations and slow movement of the planets, a few artificial satellites raced silently across the night sky. This motion reminded us that somewhere, humans were living in a high-tech world inconceivable to those eking out survival in rudimentary conditions.

I faced increasing incongruities as I became more immersed into life in Somalia. I was a self-proclaimed techno geek, loving the latest advances in electronics and computers. Yet I was drawn ever more deeply into the beauty, complexity, and interconnectedness of the natural world around me, giving a deeper awareness that advances in technology came at a cost in relationships, beliefs, and even my own identity.

"I don't believe that humans ever set foot on the moon," stated our friend Abdi matter-of-factly in one of our many conversations.

"What's so special about the moon, Abdi?" I queried.

"It's a holy place to us," he continued, asserting "all Muslims believe this!" His answer opened up a world of curiosity for me. It was one of the first real inter-faith conversations I had, and it shapes me to this day.

As a child I had seen, with my own eyes, on TV at least, the moon landing. That technological triumph was so tightly woven into my national identity I had never noticed it before. It was an arrogant assumption of my unexamined nationalistic identity. Yet, Abdi's beliefs told him that the moon was sacred to Islam and therefore was unreachable. He could not acknowledge that anyone would desecrate such a holy place.

I came away from that conversation wondering what Saudi fighter pilots believed as they raced their high-speed jets into the stratosphere. Was Abdi wrong about all Muslims believing the same thing, or did some live with deep, irreconcilable incongruities much as I, if honest, admit to having?

10

Doing and Being in Somalia

City in the Tropics

streets bleeding the stuff of the breathing
sewage, water, mango skins, banana peels
mingle as one to form the soup of our existence
afternoon rains, on the good and evil
wash the air clean of diesel and plastic
making room for the scent of flowers
sweltering heat as if the whole planet perspires
in this one in a myriad of cities with its mega malls and barrios
sweat drips from the pores of the global economy

Doing

What, exactly, did we do in Somalia? A whole mix of things, it
turns out, few of which were listed in the job description when we
signed up. MCC warned us early on in the application process that
we would have to be flexible with expectations. So, the first major
shift in expectations was from "doing things" to "being present" in
the ambiguity of what things to do. I later pontificated that flex-
ibility is one thing, but what was needed in Somalia was extreme
pliability.

The refugee camp school rehabilitation was hinted at in our job description from MCC. My role was to oversee the two-part enhancement of the school. The project included refurbishing the school building, as well as a carpentry-training component that made school desks. I worked closely with Ali Atom, a refugee hired by our predecessors. Ali taught carpentry as he oversaw the building of the school desks.

The second project we inherited was a library/typing center. Way before computers and internet forms, people needed a letter when requesting, applying, or registering for anything. The bureaucratized refugee system relied on paper forms and letters. For anyone who needed a letter typed, we provided a way to accomplish this while teaching young people to type. This program was run out of our office space and was, of course, pre-computer, so we used grit-choked typewriters. Filled in 'O's and stuck 'T's were constant maintenance items for our two portable, beat up, blue, fiberglass-covered Smith Corona Typewriters.

The third project was a small revolving business loan program. Refugees would come to our office, pitch their business plans, and receive small loans. Many of these requests, we gradually figured out, were for things more basic and short term than business startups. Medicines, school materials and food supplements were sometimes primary motivations for coming to our office to request funds. The one business we were most keen on succeeding was a bakery. The result of this business success was that we had fresh bread baked right in the camp. A small luxury even if the sweet-smelling bread usually had grit from the sandy conditions in the camp. Perhaps we were just as self-serving in our oversight of this loan program as persons who needed money for anything but the intended businesses.

A Typical Day

The cloudless sky, blue overhead, stretched from horizon to horizon. The sun beat down, causing me to squint from the reflection off the bright white sides of the Land Cruiser. The task for the day was to load finished school desks on the truck. Ali, the head carpenter, and I were to take them a mile away to the school servicing the children of the 40,000 refugees in the Saba'ad camp. Students who had gotten used to sitting on rocks in their classrooms could now have a writing surface and a more comfortable place to sit.

The desks were crafted out of discarded lumber given by the UN High Commissioner for Refugees. "Crafted" was a bit of a misnomer as was "lumber." Hacked together with inadequate, substandard hand tools was more like it. Splintered ends, misaligned nails, and rough-cut woodgrain were hazards the end-users –students!– would have to mind if they were to escape learning unscathed. Lumber was from packing crates and shipping frames that had been pulled apart, stacked, and partially rotted due to neglect on the docks where it arrived.

Still, splintery desks were better than crumbling rocks that students dragged into the classroom to sit on. When it came to school furniture, almost anything was better than a rock.

Loading school desks, product of the MCC carpentry project, to transport them to Saba'ad Refugee Camp School

To call them schools was also a bit of a misnomer. More like a long row of walls cobbled end-to-end, sitting high on a subpar block foundation, worn away by each driving monsoon rain. With gaping, frameless, holes in the walls that made up the windows and doors, these drab dirt floor block buildings were covered in noisy tin sheeting. The roof gradually became alive by the time the noonday sun cast its intensity on the building. The roof pinged and groaned loudly as it expanded in the intense heat only to sigh slightly with rapid contraction under reduced irradiation from a passing cloud.

I had a level of satisfaction on delivering finished desks. After what felt like a long and frustrating two-part project of upgrading the camp school, this felt like a finish line of sorts.

Being

Somalis used the phrase "*Inshallah*," literally "if God wills." It often irked me that they could not be more specific about attending a meeting, about getting something done, about dedicating time to seeing an idea through to completion. *Inshallah* was, I thought, used as an excuse and lack of commitment. What I learned the hard way and in retrospect, was that so many things I tried to plan were impacted by seemingly random events and people. I was not in control. The only thing I had any semblance of influence over was my own attitude. I failed miserably at that most of the time.

This struggle for adaptability sent me soul searching, best described, real time, in a letter written home.

> It has been tough to be here this last week. I'm a real bitch to live with, just ask Carolyn. She is much more resilient to this lifestyle. I thought it would be easier than it is and now that I am having a tough time, I have some disillusionment about my ideals.

Carolyn's part of this letter:

> Yes, you ask if your son's hard to live with. Well . . . uh . . . Yes, at times . . . but I still love him and hope the adjustment gets easier one of these days. I guess I don't need

as much space as Jon. If I have an hour here or there to myself, I'm OK. — September 1987 letter to Jon's parents

Much of my disillusionment, I now realize, was from being deeply unsure of my abilities to oversee the rehab/carpentry project I was to organize. In this role I had to manage a project as well as know a little something about carpentry. Having grown up tinkering in my father's wood shop, I knew a bit about crafting useful things out of wood. To the school rehabilitation part, I got mud on my shoes as a teen, mixing concrete with my father during a driveway project we did together.

I felt hopelessly inadequate in organizing a whole project that included concrete and wood. In addition, I felt cross-culturally incompetent and it showed by the number of times my anger flared, and I raised my voice in frustration. Whether loading desks on the pickup or dealing with the UN bureaucracy to secure materials, I was perpetually harried. I had little experience managing anything in my life yet, let alone people in a foreign country. In that arena, I didn't know what I didn't know.

"You are a hard man, Mr. Jon," our shop leader abruptly declared one day. I had just spouted off a string of expletives over some impediment to my plans for the day. "What do you mean by that?" I grunted, genuinely puzzled. Getting no direct answer from him, I realized, upon later reflection, that he had identified my unrealistic expectations of myself that I projected on everyone around me.

> I am glad that the school repair is over and I vowed never to do that kind of large-scale project again. It was so mentally taxing to do that project. I drove up and down the Main Street of Saba'ad 101 times and hauled 14,000 liters of water and 17 loads of sand on our truck to pour the school floor. We also put 1000 kilometers on the pickup in three weeks for this project. . . I didn't feel support from the local people who were supposed to volunteer in groups to help repair the school for their children. I have never been so angry in my life. I suppose it was just adjustment that was taking its toll but some days I was just angry all day, frustrated, with the lack of

motivation from the camp people and in blind rage at times when things went wrong. — 29 September 1987, Jon's letter to parents

Looking back, I was guilty of development aggression by forcing a project in a way that dragged people along rather than doing what I learned in college: facilitate a process of garnering ownership in a project.

A little bit of *Inshallah* would have gone a long way in settling my temperament.

Accounting

The school project opened my eyes to larger realities of what created refugees in the first place and how "taking care of them" created a whole range of other issues. In terms of development, I articulated a very first question to ask about refugees and development.

> . . . how can one do community development in a place that may not be here tomorrow? How can you motivate people who aren't living at home? —Letter to family and friends, 7 August 1987

I began to see that the international development agenda had become a business for accumulating wealth and a game of trading the power currencies of nations. Refugees were the pawns.

My experience with getting the lumber and cement used in the school rehab project proved just how much of the refugee aid was misdirected, pilfered, and generally not held accountable.

> I handed in my four-page final report on the school refurbishing project to the UNHCR. I had documented proof that it needn't take more than 150,000 shillings to repair the schools when the Somali refugee agency asked 1.5 million to do the same job. . . . it was good to have hard proof that UNHCR and their money are being abused by some of these bogus refugee provider agencies. — 29 September 1987, Jon's letter to parents

I must acknowledge that MCC provided the truck, diesel fuel, my volunteer labor, and that refugees *ended up doing* the lion's share of the work. Maybe my assessment of corruption did not account for those free inputs?

Yet how could a large organization ever do true monitoring and evaluation of their projects since the feign of accountability seemed to always come from such a surface investigation? The Somalis had a word for outsiders who "jet in, look at a project, write a report."

> We had our 1st "woofty" visit. A woofty is one who comes and visits for a day and goes home to write a report as an expert. This woofty was the deputy High Commissioner to the UNHCR. He came and went in a day or two. We had an interagency meeting with him, and he heard the complaints about how the refugees aren't getting enough nutrition or water or this or that. — Jon's letter to parents, 19 March 1987

Was I a *woofty* even though I had a bit more persistence than others I met?

International watchdog groups leveled allegations of corruption which included the widespread pilfering of the food supplies contributed by the donor community. Early in my orientation to the country, I found myself down on the docks at the port where the incoming food for refugees was received by the World Food Program (WFP). I was with an expediter who pointed out the WFP warehouse and, at the same time under his breath, discreetly pointed out another warehouse. According to him, that second warehouse was the president's. When ships laden with foodstuffs designated for refugees arrived, so the story went, half was unloaded and taken to the WFP warehouse to be transshipped to the refugee camps. The other half went to the president's warehouse to enrich him and his clan.

Other stories of government theft were more blatant.

> ... the military decided to go down to the port and take 84 brand new trucks. The people/organizations who were waiting to have their vehicles cleared, including the

Maryknoll Sisters, will just have to take a loss. Of course, the government/military promised to "look into" the matter and do something to get them back. They probably don't have a whole lot of hope. — 20 July 1987, letter sent from Djibouti to Jon's parents

That steamed me under the collar because I am keenly bothered by injustice. I knew from my research how Somalia's foreign income was disproportionately derived from refugee aid. There was little industry in the country and export of animals was the only other large revenue stream on the balance sheet. That kind of imbalanced economics made conditions ripe for corruption.

I gained some new insights on this question of corruption dynamics linked to post-colonial mentality when we took our rest and relaxation in Kenya. We stayed in the Mennonite-run Guest House. To us, this green paradise offered a relaxing time away from the sand and heat of Somalia. It was easier to reflect and gain perspective away from the intensity of our assignment in Somalia. Others found it an oasis, too. The guest house became a magnet for a diversity of people, some on the same page as us, some not.

. . . everywhere we turn, white Americans telling black Africans how to do things. We are overwhelmed by the number of missionaries here at the guesthouse this time. The audacity of people to teach Bible to those who are of such different culture that it would take 20 years to begin to understand. I'm burned out with missionaries. Yet development can be the same American telling African how to do it and I'm just as guilty. — 25 October 1987, letter from Nairobi to Jon's parents

International development was the only framework I had with which to understand what was going on in Somalia when I arrived. Studying development in college gave me a rather simplistic view of the global politicization of aid, which proved rather limited.

In the development world . . . there are good strategies and there are bad strategies. A good strategy is one where people do things for themselves and get involved in their

94

own development. They have a stake in what happens to them. The development agency acts as a facilitator. It acts as a medium between the resources and those who don't know they exist or can't get them. Of course, these theories are blown to hell in a refugee camp where everybody talks of self-sufficiency and still continues to dump tons of free things on refugees. — Letter twenty-one to Jon's parents, October 1987

In the end, my knowledge of and intentions in doing good development were not enough. The good/bad framework I used to evaluate any project provided too little nuance to understand the world. It caused me an inner dissonance to be dithering between those two extremely limited options.

Personal Adjustment Breakthrough

After all the struggles of adjustment, of reckoning my life in the camp, of deepening my commitment to trying to make a difference, I had a breakthrough in understanding myself and gaining empathy with those around me.

I have reached a new stage in my adjustment to life in the refugee camp. It has occurred to me that in the eyes of these displaced peoples we are incredibly rich. We have a relatively new truck; we have a mud brick home complete with solar lighting. We have two kerosene stoves and can buy the food we want. Most of all we have direct access to the UNHCR office. We can walk right through the swinging doors to see the sub office director without batting an eye. All Somalis are stopped at the front desk. Yet, in the Western world we are poor. Mudbrick? No generator? No food imported by Peter Justensen –a food importer firm that can get you anything– and we are relatively powerless politically. So here we are in the gap. We live in the gap. How immensely wide is the gap between the haves and have nots. I think we tend to live on the side of the haves. Yet we still live in the gap because we feel we are rich from what our Somali friends say to us. UNHCR hires national staff to live in the gap, yet they, by virtue of holding a job with the UN, are on an upwardly mobile journey. They want to be with the ranks of the haves.

MCC on the other hand encourages the downward mobile lifestyle. This makes us truly wealthy and powerful and privileged indeed when we can choose to de-accumulate or live simply. So, we try to live simply. We have placed ourselves in the camp where we can hear those who say, "you are rich and powerful." So, this is the tension I feel echoed in the many requests for money, food, kerosene, etc. We want to be a voice for the powerless, yet I feel I am failing miserably because I have not yet placed myself in a vulnerable enough position. I have not yet allowed myself to live fully in the gap. I have not yet allowed the questions to affect my behavior and lifestyle. To the extent that I will let those questions into my being, that is the extent to which I will truly be present to those I seek to serve. I am failing miserably. Yet I am here, and to a large extent cannot get away. So, there is hope that I may get beyond my own thinking future/success/ oriented world and experience the people/now/survival-oriented world. — Jon's letter to parents, April 1988

There was little time for me to relish these insights before, in a whirlwind, our adopted country imploded into civil war.

II

The End is Nigh

Three Generations of Death,
Three Generations of Hope

A drab grey cannon sits outside the high school
testament to the madness of a world at war
proud of her projectiles of death
symbol to our children might makes right

A windowless high school built as a fallout shelter
proclaiming the lunacy of the Cold-World War
form meets function in extreme efficiency
message to youth; "you have no future"

The video gaming sport of death
shoot the enemy, watch him explode
profit from playing with virtual weapons
subtle training for a warrior nation

Our Mennonite grandfathers resisted the draft
meek opposition to the face of global pyre
heritage that said no to death and yes to life
paving the way by their witness

Our Mennonite fathers marched in the streets
speaking truth to insanity

hammering bombs as an act of creation
doing time in jail for protest; the crucible of hope

As a Mennonite father will I resist
the slow march of soldiering youth
toward the rigidity of thinking
that guns make peace?

In addition to my project-related stresses, political instability took an emotional toll. The constant inner tensions caused by rumors of wars, expulsions of expatriates, and the sea of corruption threatened to swamp my ability to cope.

It was early on that I found it necessary to interact with the Somali military. Needing permission to leave Hargeisa to go to the refugee camp, I wrote this in my journal:

> I found myself in a room full of military men, many had guns. I just wanted a vehicle pass to allow me to travel from Hargeisa and our project at Saba'ad Camp. Yet here I was, surrounded by all the earthly power Somalia has to offer. What was my response? I only came away questioning how my pacifism could have anything to say to these men. There was not only the power mentality difference, but the cross-cultural barriers to our communication. Like a good passive pacifist, I observed, not only them, but myself. How do I react to this power? Rubbing shoulders with this power sometimes sets up false expectations and hopes. I am uncomfortable with guns. Soldiers have solved conflict with them for years. So, I got my pass and left. But the questions have not left me. — Journal entry, March 1987

GI Joe

It was the final days of Somalia intact as a nation state in the spring of 1988 when I was one of the last people to leave the Hargeisa airport after dropping someone off for the daily Somali Airlines flight. I noticed some men looking out of place standing around and engaged them in conversation only to discover that they were

US Marines waiting for a ride that obviously was not showing up. Hesitant at first to be identified in any way to the US military, I decided it was more important to be neighborly and give them a ride into town than to hide behind my principles of strict separation from military. Upon further gentle probing, I discovered that they were there to, according to the commander, "improve the Somalian (sic) military." I so desperately wanted to take them to the refugee camp where I worked and wave my hand over the 40,000 war and economic refugees from Ethiopia and say, "see what an improved military does."

It was no more than a few months later that the very guns these Marines were sent to service killed civilians in Somalia's civil war. Those 105 mm Jeep mounted Howitzers leveled the city of Hargeisa and blew up our fuel stored in the UNHCR compound.

Birth of a Dictator

In October 1969, Mohamed Siad Barre took over governance of Somalia in a bloodless coup, setting up his administration based on the model of scientific socialism. His program: bring Somalia into contemporary times through educational, social, and economic advancements. One example of this modernization was a literacy campaign in 1973 and 1974 that codified the yet to be written Somali language.

Barre's scientific socialism, during the height of the Cold War, saw the country leaning toward the Soviet Union. Somalia received copious amounts of aid from the USSR as a proxy state in the Cold War. The US countered in the Horn of Africa by arming Ethiopia. Cold War political schizophrenia insured that Somalia remained an expendable pawn.

Another of Barre's goals: the unification of all Somali-speaking people in the region. As a first attempt at unification, he launched an attack on Ethiopia in November 1977 to capture the Ogaden region and incorporate it back into Somalia. Being repulsed by the switch of alliances by the cold-war overlords, the

Somali army retreated. With Ethiopia now supported by USSR, Somalia fell under the spell of US foreign policy.

Barre's leadership, frustrated in his attempts to unify all Somalis, degenerated into repression, fear, and paranoia. He outlawed any talk of tribes, clans, and family allegiances which countered his focus on building a cohesive nation state; he nevertheless biased all country resources to keep him in power. As twilight fell on his long, ruthless reign as president-for-life, Siad Barre's governance hardened into a classic case of divide and rule. The long-term effect of this approach was mounting animosity with increasingly repressive tactics needed to keep a lid on the growing resentment. Bolstered by a dreaded Soviet-style secret police called the National Security Service (NSS), Barre developed an extensive network of agents who reported any dissent. Foreigners involved in development, justice, and refugees were under suspicion as they reported human rights abuses to Amnesty International and other rights groups.

> In the northwest the military and authorities are southern tribespeople appointed by the president. While all the northerners are other tribes. The military general of the northwest has decided to commit economic genocide in the northwest fearing their rebellion. That's it in a nutshell. The organizations such as MCC, AFSC, Save the Children, Islamic relief and others work under these conditions, never knowing when all-out war will break.
> — 20 July 1987, letter sent from Djibouti to Jon's parents

Once I was picked up by the NSS and interrogated. A plain white car loaded with soldier types stopped me on a city street and demanded to know who I was. They commanded me to go to the NSS compound and grilled me about what I was doing in Hargeisa, my organizational affiliation, and why I was walking on the street. It was unheard of for NGO personnel to be out of their vehicles, just walking. For a brief, extremely unnerving moment, the NSS interrogator had my passport in his grasp. This small blue booklet with the US eagle on the front, I realized later, gave me a false bravado and sense of exceptionalism. Stripped of that, I felt vulnerable, almost naked, a flash of insight as to what it might be like to be a refugee, destitute and without a country. In the end they let me go with a reprimand to not be walking on the "dangerous" streets.

Also, during this time, palpable tensions between the local population and southern occupiers burst into the open with regularity. Since I was working with the refugees, I was identified with the occupiers. In addition to calling me "*gall*" or infidel, children picking up their parents' disgust at outsiders often threw rocks at me while I was riding a motorcycle through the Hargeisa city streets.

Tensions were constant and slowly increasing, bringing the political situation to a boil. The national government had a habit of flexing its muscles by conducting low level over-flights of Hargeisa with their ancient MIG 17s and 19s. Way out of compliance with European aircraft safety requirements, these ancient Soviet warbirds terrorized the city with their deafening roar as they streaked low overhead.

With each new bit of news predicting wars and rumors of wars, I absorbed and re-emitted the cold sweat of anxiety, reinforcing the doom around me. That intense anxiety made me realize I had not tapped into the life force necessary to do the peace work I was so passionate about.

Sounds of the End

Tense signs of the unraveling were everywhere. Military personnel in fatigues. Checkpoints demanding papers, harassing people as they moved about in the daytime. Curfews from dusk to dawn.

Lying in bed in Hargeisa one night, I heard automatic weapon fire. It was a full-fledged gun battle somewhere in the pitch black outside my bedroom window. I could tell there were multiple weapons firing from different directions like a call-and-response in a church service. It was as if the fight was a rational conversation. You fire, I fire back. As with most passionate and emotional verbal interactions, sometimes both were speaking at the same time. In this case many joined simultaneously, each raising their "voices" louder and longer, emptying their clips faster with longer bursts.

Rifles make different sounds depending on where they are pointed when fired. Bullets shot vertically in the air give a different report than ones shot horizontally toward something solid.

I learned that lesson one night hearing five single shots that sounded similar with the whizzing hyper-sonic ballistic slug echoing off into the darkness. The sixth shot had a different quality, a more subdued report, with more of a dull, muffled thud sound. I learned the next day that a prominent townsman had been shot and killed at a checkpoint after five warning shots.

It took me a while to understand that not all shots fired were at me. Yet who can risk not ducking with each crack or boom? And sometimes the barrels *were* really pointed at me.

Cresting the hill on the familiar road into Hargeisa, I abruptly came upon a new checkpoint I had never before encountered. Soldiers taut with fear pointed their guns at my truck. A quick scan revealed one soldier prone on the road with an AK-47, one in the bushes with his finger on the trigger of a rocket propelled grenade, and several more at various other points scattered around. All had me in their cross hairs.

This heightened alert came from a rebel attack just days before. A Land Rover, looking very much like Grover, had feigned as an official military vehicle. As it approached the government checkpoint, the rebels popped up from the back and mowed down the government soldiers at this same checkpoint. My arrival made them think another attack was imminent. I emerged from that standoff physically intact but shaken.

Shortly before Somalia joined the fraternity of so-called "failed states," we ventured out of our walled Hargeisa compound for the evening, trying to conduct life as normally as possible. Although there was a curfew that started at eight pm, we couldn't stand being cooped up in the house any longer, night after night. So, we went to a restaurant for dinner and accidentally stayed out past eight pm. As we navigated our Land Cruiser from the restaurant back to our house through darkened narrow dirt streets, we encountered a hidden checkpoint. A soldier shoved a Kalashnikov in our face as we approached shouting for us to stop. I saw that this soldier was a child, no more than eleven or twelve years old. For the briefest of moments before we turned off the headlights and flicked on the dome light, his face was illuminated, revealing terror. His fear was as real and jumpy as mine. For that moment, he held our lives in the small of his trigger finger. Seeing we were no threat, he let us pass but this encounter added to my accumulating trauma.

Soul Searching

We are just a sack of gooey liquid, kept together by a thin pliable covering of skin, held up by marrow and sinew. The often-titanic forces at play all around in the physical world can squash even the most muscular physique. We are all just miniscule, fragile creatures under the shadow of a volcano, tsunami, or typhoon. What horrific and devastating destruction does our species first imagine, then bring to being through weapons developed to project power? How common have these instruments of death become!

In the house where I stayed in Hargeisa was a chunk of blackened, jagged, razor-sharp metal. Picked up by the previous residents, it was a half-pound piece of shrapnel from a howitzer shell or fragment grenade. Traveling at ballistic speeds when exploded, it was designed to shred stone and steel and flesh. Holding that piece of flak amazed and baffled me. How can humans put their creative energies into such anti-human designs?

I have observed how sounds leave a vibrational imprint. The human-made soundscapes of Northwest Somalia left an imprint of fear on me. These contrast to the natural sounds of wind, water, and trees which calm my mind into the tranquility I described in the chapters above.

In places of chaos, when fear is the primary vibrational frequency, guns and shovels are equal implements for employment. One "tool" renders the living lifeless. The other buries "ashes to ashes, dust to dust." And sometimes, they cost the same amount of money. After the civil war raged full force in Mogadishu, young men could pick up a knockoff AK-47 for ten bucks. Join a militia. Make a living. If they chose a shovel, join the grave diggers, make a living. All this living on the backs of the dying. The impact of violence doesn't end with the laying down of guns.

The Thud of a Coconut

Like the imprints of battle on the souls of combat veterans, the violence I encountered in Somalia left indelible marks on my person. For years upon returning to the US, I subconsciously and through muscle memory straddled potholes when driving, avoiding places where there may be a landmine. I had an involuntary physical reaction to loud sounds, while fireworks sounded too much like gunfire. Years later, I noticed similar reactions by community members in a place often visited by violence.

In May 2013 I was leading a group of students on a learning tour to a community in the Autonomous Region of Muslim Mindanao in the southern Philippines. My goal, on that sultry day, was to hear how they were transforming the violence that had plagued them for the past forty years.

We were sitting in the shade of their open-air community meeting space. All of a sudden there was the deep thud made by a falling coconut. In a fraction of a second, I observed in some of those around me, the briefest impulse to jump, drop or duck for cover. In that split second, a paralyzing disorientation and confusion flashed like white lightning before my eyes as if the wave of fear was infectious and spread instantaneously. But that all passed in a heartbeat and the conversation proceeded with half the group, the students, not noticing the phenomena. The other half, those in the community who had past experience with gunfire, reacted to the coconut thud with protective reflexes. Unfortunately, this reflex is all too common in areas of the world where conflict regularly boils into violence.

Leaving with Providence

Carolyn and I left northern Somalia on the last commercial flight in 1988, just seventeen hours before the sack of Hargeisa. I admit to feeling regret and guilt for not having stayed to witness the destruction of the city as my foreign colleagues did. As a pacifist who has gotten a glimpse of the ugly reality of armed conflict, it is hard to admit my mixed emotions of that which I abhor: war. In a newsletter we drafted on 7 June 1988 in Nairobi, Kenya, I described dealing with both the guilt of leaving our staff in Hargeisa as well as our co-worker who was later evacuated by the United Nations.

> Some call it fate, some call it Providence, and some call it a miracle, but it happened about three times to us a week ago. Maybe some of you have heard of the fighting in northwest Somalia on the US media. We narrowly escaped being pinned down by the fighting and shelling of the town of Hargeisa.
>
> On May 27, 1988, the SNM (Somali National Movement of the northern Isaaq tribe of Somalis who had been fighting on and off for the last ten years and wanting to upset the regime in Mogadishu of Saied Barre, president) stormed into the town of Burco, a border town about 100 miles east of Hargeisa. They killed the military general, the leader of the local "KGB" type agency and the governor, all of whom were from the southern tribes. The SNM claimed to have captured the town and were going to take more of the North. On that day, we were in camp and were going to leave for Hargeisa and Mogadishu in a few days to go on our holiday to Nairobi with my folks. When we heard the news from our workers, they said it nonchalantly and we passed it off.
>
> The SNM hate for Barre was surpassed only by their ability to exaggerate their claims, at least in the past. When we heard that there was a curfew on the road that runs by camp and goes into Hargeisa, we thought, "well expats always get through." I took our employee to near Hargeisa. I was the only vehicle on the road, but the four checkpoints we had to go through to get to Hargeisa were calm, and the soldiers waved us by. They were more

heavily armed than usual. That day we saw thick black smoke from the airport which we later learned was one of their MIGs that crashed after they forced it to take off when not airworthy. The next day we decided to go to Hargeisa a bit early, like in the morning instead of afternoon as we had earlier planned.

We got to Hargeisa and went straight to a UN security briefing. They said that the city was sealed off for the next while and no exceptions and they also announced a 3:00 PM curfew on the town. We also learned that the only airplane that goes to Mogadishu was broken down in Djibouti. So, we kind of worried about making it out to Kenya on time. Our only option was to fly to Djibouti, so we made it to the ticket office just before it closed and got a ticket for the next day, Monday 30 May, and packed. Next morning, we went to the airport and left.

From Djibouti one must go through Addis Ababa to get to Nairobi, and that's what we did. On Tuesday in Djibouti, we heard the fighting started in Hargeisa about 12 hours after we left and then on Wednesday, we learned that Hargeisa had been taken.

On Thursday we learned that all the expats in Hargeisa were evacuated by three chartered UN planes. Our own coworker, Deb, was among the evacuees. We have learned that she has gotten to Mogadishu okay and that they were indeed pinned down for a few days, and under artillery fire . . . from whose side it is unclear.

Even to this day the government claims that all is calm and under government control, in all the northwest. It refuses to admit that there was fighting and that it lost some cities. Now because the government is embarrassed about the evacuation, they gave all the evacuees 48 hours to get back to their assignment or get out of the country.

We are not sure of our assignment in the northwest, we are not even sure if we will be allowed to get back into Somalia. One thing we are sure of is that the refugees are suffering. Some of the camps in the northwest had water hauled by truck and the food, if not already looted, was probably taken by the military. So, if we had stayed in the camp, I seriously think we would be very hungry by now.

People we know/knew are now dead because many of the "office" and "bureaucratic" people we worked with in Hargeisa were southerners and no matter who comes out on top in the end, south or north, people will die.

Even if we can go back to our assignment, we will have to start over and do relief type of work. It leaves kind of a sick feeling in my stomach. If you want to work for peace, stop the small arms trade, it is a much worse threat to the 3rd world than nuclear buildup.

We also learned after coming to Kenya that some acquaintances from Somalia were the ones killed in the bomb blast in Khartoum a few weeks ago. All 4 of the family were killed, including 2 children.

I realize that these "terrorist" actions bring out a rage and anger in me that is, in itself, the root cause for the type of violence of today's world. Unless I can truly learn to love those, who shoot at me, those who blow up my friends, I am, to a much lesser extent, but still, I am just like the perpetrators of such violence. My cause must be peace, my methods must be personal integrity, social justice and finding a support community that believes that peace is possible.

It has been good to be with other MCCers and Mennonites here in Nairobi. We have felt support and understanding from those who have been in similar situations in Sudan, Ethiopia, and elsewhere in Africa. Thank you all for your support. — Newsletter, 7 June 1988 in Nairobi, Kenya

We had no problems when we returned to Mogadishu on 26 June 1988. After Carolyn had a bout with typhoid and six-week convalescence in Kenya, we were reassigned to Kismayo, a southern city along the Indian Ocean coastline.

Salvaging Our Term of Service

In a newsletter to family and friends we described our ongoing questions, struggles and attempts to fulfill our commitment to a full three-year term of service with MCC.

It is very discouraging to think that our confiscated vehicles with the MCC emblem on the door –the dove of peace and the cross– might be running around with soldiers packed in them shooting people.

This is a very stressful time for us. Our future is uncertain, we have been yanked up from our home and are living out of two suitcases, we're uncertain if our Somali friends are alive or dead and we know nothing of the northwest as rumors and half-truths are running rampant in Somalia. No accurate information is to be had and even in the capital of Somalia the truth is not known or told. —Newsletter to family and friends, March 1989

We had a plan to go back to Hargeisa a year after we fled the north. In mid-1989, the UNHCR had a plan to reregister the newly displaced persons in the northwest, but that fell through with renewed fighting. I desired intensely to get back to Hargeisa and the north, really feeling like I was ripped away from that area prematurely.

We eventually were reassigned to continue some work started by some Mennonite volunteers who ended their term. This was in the southern port city of Kismayo. In the same newsletter we described trying to carry on with our term.

Some of you have asked for a clear description of our new jobs. Although MCC Somalia still has people placed in the southern refugee camps, Jon and I are not working with refugees. Instead, we are working with the Ministry of Health (MOH) and the United Nations Children's Fund (UNICEF) in the delivery of Primary Health care to the southern region where we live. It's sort of set up like this: UNICEF provides the funding for the program, MOH decides how the money will be used — spend it all on cars or divided among the various sections of Primary Health Centers such as immunization, health teaching, sanitation for example — and MCC provides two willing workers to work with both parties. So, we go to the MOH building each morning to see what, if anything, is going on. Officially Jon is assigned to work with the sanitation on latrine/water issues and I am to work with the training officer on health training programs. Another part of our job for MCC is to gather information about health practices of the nomadic population so that if and when MOH/UNICEF attempts to provide consistent health care to this group, MCC can work as advocates to preserve the culture instead of replacing it, as so often happens with nomadic people. At this point the healthcare delivery system for settled people is so fragile we can't imagine MOH/UNICEF will be involved with nomads during our stay here. — Newsletter to family and friends, March 1989

While it was peaceful at first in Kismayo, the expanding civil war was fast encroaching on all areas of the country.

Take Down the Flag: Working Alongside the UN

It was a typical sweltering day in Kismayo, Somalia. The breezes off the coast just a few hundred yards away did little to alleviate the humid heat. Carolyn and I were attempting once more to find meaningful work in a country that was fast collapsing in on itself from a spreading civil war. Twenty years of divide and rule by then-President Barre were catching up with him. We had already been chased from the northern part of the country due to a full-scale civil war, which started in May 1988. Now seconded to both the Ministry of Health and UNICEF, we were trying to salvage our MCC volunteer term in the deep south of this Horn of Africa nation-state.

As tensions mounted in the country, we met with NGOs working in Kismayo to plan for our extrication should things turn sour in the south as they had in the north. The Italian Air Force contingent at the airport outside of town had offered to ferry us foreigners to the capital, Mogadishu, a one-hour flight, should fighting begin in the city. But just days after this commitment, we saw their C-130 aircraft fly north, never to return. That contingency plan was useless.

The UN had little influence in the country. Its huge staff, massive infrastructure, and vast task of feeding and caring for refugees made it that much more vulnerable to the whims of the Barre regime. The other UN agencies like UNDP, UNICEF, and others were even more susceptible since they had even less bargaining power with national and local authorities. We had one last personal example of UN impotency in Kismayo.

We checked in regularly with the UNICEF office and the uptight French national who was in charge of the Kismayo sub-office. On one particular morning, he was absent from the city when we arrived at the office. We found that the local police had entered the office and demanded the two-way radio microphone from the local staff, suspecting they were somehow spying on the local populace. When the Frenchman heard of this breech of UN protocol, he radioed us and told us to "take down the flag." Now, Carolyn and I were only seconded to UNICEF, not actual UN employees, so we had no authority to remove the UN flag from the compound and it didn't seem to be our job, so we refused.

UN offices and compounds supposedly have diplomatic immunity to local laws. The removal of the UN flag from a UN compound is a statement that something has contravened this immunity and become an event of international significance. For the local UNICEF office director, the removal of the flag was his only way to exert what little authority he had over the UN jurisdiction assigned him. It seemed a futile attempt at influence and control with, what we know now, would be a final national meltdown.

Failing Banks and Last Withdrawal of Cash From Kismayo Bank

The last time I withdrew money from the bank in Somalia, before the total implosion into civil war, I mounted the dusty steps of the central bank building on a sleepy street in the southern Somali port town of Kismayo. Wars and rumors of wars swirled through the grapevine among expats. Word of war on the streets and among foreign NGO workers made us all nervous of the unraveling of normalcy or what passed for such. One impending household crisis was a lack of cash to buy any food or supplies.

Entering the empty, dark bank building, doors flung wide open due to the heat and lack of electricity, I took my passbook, presented it to the only teller around. It was a creepy, ghost town atmosphere with obviously no one having used the bank in days if not weeks. Saying I needed to withdraw money so I could go to the market to buy something to eat, the teller shrugged and said it was impossible. I pled with him, pointing at my positive bank balance in the record book. He seemed undeterred in his apathy. My pleading drew the bank manager into the one-sided conversation and, upon explaining my predicament, he grabbed me by the elbow and escorted me down the steps. I was perplexed. We got in a taxi that wound its way through the dusty streets, stopping in front of an ordinary shop. The manager introduced me to his brother, the shop owner. After a curt conversation between the two, the shop owner reached under the counter and with a "whump" slammed down a foot-thick stack of Somali shillings, one-hundred dollars equivalent, on the counter. Relieved to have some cash, that was the last withdrawal I ever made from a Somali bank.

The collapsing economy of Somalia tracked by the deteriorating political situation, created an untenable financial situation for most Somalis. Hyper-inflation meant that even stacks of cash were nearly worthless. How do you buy a car, for example, when the largest currency note in a cash-based economy is only worth the equivalent of ten US cents? Not that most Somalis had that kind of liquid wealth, but even buying cattle or camels, for example, demanded a wheelbarrow full of money.

So it was that economic, political, and finally social collapse descended on Somalia. In the end, MCC left because it had racked up five vehicle losses to theft and abandonment. Mobility was crucial to security in rural programs, so MCC halted the whole country program due to lack of vehicles.

The decision to close the program was inevitable. We spent the last week in the country burning files and giving away the furnishings of the Mogadishu team house.

The Last Day

I was desperate to get on that plane. I was frantic after nearly three years of tension, anxiety, and outright trauma as the nation state of Somalia collapsed. Carolyn and I had booked a flight on Kenya Airways, finally leaving the country for good. Moving through the chaos outside the Mogadishu Airport to get to the boarding stage, we knew from experience, wore us out like a full day's hard labor.

First, we had to navigate from the parking lot past the beggars, street kids, and incessant baggage handlers grabbing at our luggage. Then, balancing checked bags and carry-ons, we had to produce proof to the soldiers guarding the front door that it was *our* plane we had come to the airport to board, as if anyone would intentionally go through this insanity for the fun of it. Once past the security cordon, we entered the crowded and boisterous mayhem of passengers, their families, and well-wishers who packed the departure hall. That no queue of any sort existed for the check-in process rankled my ordered sensibilities and forced me enter the fray to push my way toward the ticket agent while Carolyn, standing in a less congested area, minded the luggage.

With one last, exhausted burst of energy, I wiggled through the packed lobby and up to the airline check-in desk. Shoulder to shoulder against the counter, my long arm threaded through the bodies to wave our tickets at the airline agent. I was relieved when our tickets were grabbed. We would soon be on our way. The airline representative who held our tickets, looked at our names, then scanned her list. Then she more thoroughly searched the list again.

As if out of body, I heard her say, "The plane is full. You will have to go Wednesday."

"What?" I said, confused. "We have a reservation!"

"You are not on my passenger manifest," she said flatly.

"But see, we have a tickets!" I announced, stabbing the paper-thin means of escape with my finger. "Check your list again!" I demanded with rising indignation.

"No, sorry," she countered after feigning another look at the printout.

Wednesday? I thought anxiously. *I won't make it that long. Can't you see I am close to a meltdown?* I screamed in my head.

"You gave our reservations to someone else . . . for a bribe I bet," I blurted out, louder than I intended.

I saw the "NO!" harden in her posture and on her face.

Damn, I thought despondently. *Now I've done it. We'll never get on that plane today.*

I staggered back from the counter now glaring a short distance away at her. The gulf between our positions was widening, literally and figuratively. In my head I shouted; *I want on!* Her silent glare responded, *You will not get on!*

And we didn't. It was another three nerve-wracking days, holed up in some friend's house before we finally left the country. During that anxious wait, Somalia would slide further into the abyss of civil war. Tensions on the streets of Mogadishu, bombings downtown, and gunfire at night eroded my mental footing further.

A lifetime of introspection since has given me some insights on that terse, yet critical exchange at the airline ticket counter in the Mogadishu airport. At the end of my rope, I think my unrealistic expectations about how I, as a lone individual, could positively impact the world finally collapsed. The last straw was failing miserably in even leaving the country with poise.

I am not an island. I needed help from the ticket agent, and yet my actions reeked with bravado, privilege, and exceptionalism. I had a problem and should have asked for her help, been vulnerable with my needs. My accusation of bribery, however much truth there might have been in that statement, wounded her dignity in the same way a physical injury would. The research in my field of peacebuilding reveals that wounded dignity is behind much of the ongoing pain and trauma in the world today. I added to the collective brokenness that day. I now see how little inner fortitude I had, how little foundation I had to do the good I wanted.

I left Somalia for the last time, in October 1989, a frazzled mess.

12

Postscript

The Truth of Change

Fake news all day now
What do we make of this change?
Traditions shifted

DESPITE THE TURBULENT BEGINNINGS and burned-out endings of those years in Somalia, I am still drawn to the Horn of Africa by some compelling force. It's a siren song calling me back, promising to fill an empty void, complete something uncompleted, or fulfill a longing I can't quite name from that era of my life. What an odd reaction, since I left Somalia an emotional wreck. In retrospect, perhaps it is my connection to the pure physicality of the place: the sensual memories of sound and smell and taste provide the soothing balm that tempers the pain.

In the intervening years the Somali experience compelled me into a deeper search for spiritual and personal grounding. By the time I had the opportunity to travel back decades later, I had reflected, grown and healed from the trauma of those first years.

POSTSCRIPT

Going Back

The first of my eight trips back to Somaliland in the current era was in March 2013, twenty-five years after we left on that last flight out of Hargeisa. I had been invited to the University of Hargeisa's Institute of Peace and Conflict Studies (IPCS) to give short seminars on topics of peacebuilding and conflict transformation. Establishing a relationship with the IPCS and facilitating some courses on peace seemed, by my own reckoning anyway, to balance the equation in my own head about any harm I may have contributed to when I was there in the 80s. I could support the betterment of the nation now.

One of the first things I did after settling into the Hargeisa guesthouse on that first trip was listen to a Phil Collins play list. It was those same songs that moved my heart then in the 1980s as now. That playlist with Collins crooning about love, fame, and all that was in vogue in the 80s looped over and over and over on a cassette tape as a touchstone to the Western culture I had left behind in 1987.

Playing those songs in 2013 was cathartic. I sat on the guest house rooftop overlooking the university. My damp eyes looked beyond the campus walls, toward the dry plastic-strewn valley that cut Hargeisa in half. I traced the route we traveled so often up the other side of the hill to where our MCC house used to stand.

On my final trip back to Hargeisa in March of 2020, when this book draft was well underway, I held the wispy thin aerograms I saved from the 80s between my fingers in the dim light of a Somaliland evening. As the call to prayer echoed through the minarets scattered throughout the city, I was acutely aware that that ancient call had remained a constant. The same then as now. As if no time had passed at all. The past as the present, full circle. Continuity.

Can ghosts inhabit paper? If so, then I held these specters in my hands, the type-written letters. On them was revealed so much about me, all those many years ago. Taking these letters back to Somalia in 2020 completed a circle of connection. These fragile old letters held words I had crafted thirty-three years ago, to the day, in this very location.

Ageing and remembering is a funny thing. The way that Somalia has shaped my thinking has become a reference point; it is always in the background of my mind. That time in Somalia has haunted me: a cacophony of senses, voices on the wind, the movement in the corner of my vision, and the ever-present scent of the desert winds just below my consciousness.

It meant living with the decades of incompleteness and unfinished business with our unplanned flight during the civil war. It's as if that Phil Collins playlist needed to be aired out loud, those aerograms read and handled in that space one more time to put the close bracket on my Somali sojourn. As I sat on the roof top playing those songs, I wept. In the tears were all the ghosts of the people and the places and the has-beens and the should-have-beens. I was weeping for my incompetence, the incompleteness, the intolerance, and all the information that was never fully mine.

Where are the People?

What endures from my Mennonite clan's fifty-plus years of working in the Horn of Africa is remarkably simple. It is relationships. Mennonites spent time with Somali clans asking the quite simple questions that begin relationships: Who are you? What's important to you? Tell us how we can be of assistance.

After all the donated tractors of development have been buried by the sands of time, relationships endure. Relationships built, honoring the dignity of the other, respect, and trust remain well beyond the sunset of the latest trend in development.

The final result of some well-intended project

This is what I ardently believe. Yet, here is a confession as I worked through writing the chapters for this memoir. I am reminded of something that has disturbed me ever since I left Somalia. Where are the people in my story? Where is the telling of Somalis who inhabited that land and with whom I had relationships while there? Where are their perspectives? Why are their comments so sparse when my life's work has been peacebuilding which is all about relationships and people-centered security? Where are the people?

As I pondered that time of my life, thirty-two months on the ground in East Africa, I came to a few conclusions. First, is the reality that MCC in Somalia was beholden to big organizations, like the UN, to operate there. The logistics of security necessitated big, heavy, and expensive infrastructures. For communication to far-flung corners of the country, high-frequency radios were used. For local, city-wide communications, they utilized VHF radio networks. There were no cell phones and landlines; it was only midterm when we were there that MCC got its first telephone in the office. The mail service was weak to non-existent, so we relied on the UN mail pouch system to send letters and documents throughout the country. The UN provided an umbrella agreement under which MCC was able to secure permissions for movement throughout the country, work permits, and most essentially, visas to enter and reside in the country. All of these logistical realities would have been impossible to develop and navigate on our own with the small budget MCC allotted the country program.

By nature, the UN focuses on program, policy, and logistics first, with people coming in second in priority. They value rules and procedures over humans. The UN was already entangled in the political machinations of the day, so it was often reacting to the latest attempt by Barre to control it and the resources the UN had access to.

Layer on top of that the logistical complexity needed to operate in a violence-prone social system. That insulative layer impeded outsiders from deep and abiding relationships with Somali people. Somalis also had a rugged independent nomadic mentality which was inherently distrustful of outsiders, further impeding genuine relationships with us. That meant that years of interaction were necessary before trust could develop. The Eastern Mennonite Missions presence, focused exclusively and long term in the south, had developed close relationships with some persons. But MCC was operating in the UN sphere of influence, so these long-term relationships did not transfer to the work among refugees. Finally, the disparity in money and resources as well as initial lack of linguistic fluency meant that I had no clue what was going on, let alone the ability to develop close relationships.

All those justifications, I will freely admit, is why the sand of Somalia has scratched so many guilty lines in my psyche. It is what has propelled me back to Somaliland all these years later to maybe undo some of the damage I inadvertently caused by lack of human engagement then.

Finally, however, I must admit that the lack of significant relationships with Somalis during my nearly three years there is why the memories have been such a burden to carry all these years. I see now that this writing has more to do with learning the importance of relationships by their absence. My truth is that I developed more significant relationships in successive MCC terms, both because of different, more welcoming cultures, and because I became more vulnerable and transparent in my need for friendships.

The memoirs of Carolyn's and my time in Swaziland — now called Eswatini — and Philippines, if they ever get written, will be much more about the characters and relationships that were formed in those places. In Eswatini, from 1992 to 1997, we connected with a Swazi family for a home stay, grounding our time in a relationship of belonging. They gave us names and called us their family. In the Philippines from 2001 to 2007, I worked shoulder to shoulder with Filipinos who gave their lives to building peace. This solidarity with colleagues has so far spanned twenty-two years and keeps me returning yearly.

Over the years as I reflected on being dunked headfirst into the unfamiliar realities, be they vastly different world views or geopolitical meddling in local power dynamics, it dawned on me that development was not as simple and straightforward as I thought. When I confronted the limits of my intentions, my sense of self was uprooted. I grasped that altruism, which I thought motivated me, was not the end all and be all of what motivated people in desperate situations. That stark realization put me on a quest for a more complete understanding of the world. That search motivated me to study peace. This time though, my scholastic pursuits at seminary, graduate certificates in conflict transformation and teaching for higher education, were tempered with experience beyond just head knowledge.

Finally

I arrived in Somalia in early 1987 with such optimistic naivete. I left less than three years later with my tail between my legs, whimpering and disoriented at the enormity of the global dysfunction I had witnessed. A final exchange with the airline agent as I attempted to leave the country embodied all that I saw wrong with the world, everything that was wrong in me. In honesty and the clarity of self-reflection, it was I who added to, not healed, the brokenness.

In a way, my direct experience with violence and nonviolence in Somalia became a focus for my intellectual curiosity for the next decades. As I explored these themes, I uncovered my engagement with violence and nonviolence which was integral to my life from nearly the beginning.

It is deeply unfair for me to give the impression that there was only war and famine and flooding and upheaval in Somalia. The international media does way too much of that already. My experiences were deeply formational and sometimes traumatizing. Through them I have a deeper understanding of self and the world and in that way, they are a gift.

That said, I cannot seem to get away from this place in the Horn of Africa. I think I have discovered what compels me to return all these years later: I believe it is the sand strewn by a thousand nights, ten thousand hallucinations bombarding my senses, and a million stories of survival. I welcome that I still have a hole in my heart and sand in my shoes from this wonderful, terrible place.

I set forth in writing this tome to launch me into the new and the next, and to set my sights on the horizon. I'm grateful to Somalia and Somalis for the sand in my shoes that won't come out. With the writing of this book, I have now come to be at peace with the ever-present granules reminding me that I am connected to people and places far away. That sand provides a grounding and fills me with gratitude for a part of the world which has polished me so profoundly.

Sunset from our home in the refugee camp